Map of the area, 1792.

WESTON-SUPER-MARE
PAST

View from Knightstone to Worlebury, *c*.1850.

WESTON-SUPER-MARE
PAST

Philip Beisly

Phillimore

2001

Published by
PHILLIMORE & CO. LTD.
Shopwyke Manor Barn, Chichester, West Sussex

ISBN 1 86077 174 2

Printed and bound in Great Britain by
BIDDLES LTD.
Guildford, Surrey

Contents

List of Illustrations

Frontispiece: View from Knightstone to Worlebury, *c*.1850.

Acknowledgements

Raymond Dwerryhouse, 2, 71; Andrew Eddy, 5, 72-4, 143; Helicopter Museum, 117, 129;
North Somerset Museum Service, 7, 9, 10, 13, 15, 16, 26, 42, 44, 45, 47, 49, 52, 57, 58, 67,
79, 80, 90, 92-7, 103, 115, 125-7, 133-5; Mr. Sloman, 39-41; Howard Smith, 33, 113; Sharon
Poole, 106; Weston Library, 45; Weston Mercury, 118-21, 141.

Introduction

This book traces the story of Weston-super-Mare. The principal interest lies in the growth and character of the Victorian resort, for Britain invented the seaside and Weston-super-Mare is a classic example of the British watering place. However, this part of the story is only the centrepiece, and the book traces the settlement's older history and its more recent past.

I am grateful to those who have read and commented on the text: Mary Harding, Robert Smart and Martin Taylor. Nicholas Corcos gave me guidance on Weston's early history, and Dr. Peter Miller supplied useful information on the local quarrying industry. I have also profited from numerous conversations with Brian Austin, covering many aspects of the town's story. I received kind assistance from North Somerset Museum Service, Chris Richards, the *Weston Mercury*, Councillor Elfan ap Rees, and the Somerset County Records Office, and also from Mr. John Bailey, Mr. Clive Jackson and Mr. Michael Woods of Woodspring District Council. I owe a large debt of gratitude to the staff of Weston Central Library; the Library's Local History Room contains a rich store of guidebooks, maps, newspapers and periodicals, local government records, and the local census returns.

I am conscious of a more general debt of gratitude to all those with whom, at various times, I have discussed the story of Weston-super-Mare: I have probably stored up many facts and ideas from these conversations which I am now producing as my own without acknowledgement. Any omissions of this kind are unintentional, and any errors are my own.

Chapter One

Early History

MOST MODERN VISITORS to Weston-super-Mare approach the town across the great plain of the Northmarsh, the northern section of the Somerset Levels, and see the mass of Worle Hill rising like an island. It was indeed an island at times in the pre-historic past, when sea levels were higher and the waters of the Severn Estuary reached many miles farther inland than they do today. Even when the modern coastline had become stabilised and sand dunes had formed to consolidate it, much of the Northmarsh was a swampy terrain drained by sluggish streams and rivers. It was only when the village of Weston was already turning into a resort, in the early years of the 19th century, that the draining of this landscape, pursued down the centuries of recorded history, was brought to completion. The village which the early visitors discovered at the end of the 19th century was still an isolated settlement clinging to the hillside.

Worle Hill is largely carboniferous lime-stone, and is an outcrop of the rock forming the main mass of the Mendip Hills. Limestone country has an ancient feeling; its clean line brings one close to the rock beneath, which outcrops constantly and lies about the surface. The contrast between this upland scenery and the surrounding levels makes the hills seem higher than they are. The historian Collinson described Worlebury in 1791:

> This mountain is an immense rock of lime-stone, with but very little herbage intermixed; yet here and there a solitary sheep is seen pasturing on its naked, barren ridge, which, being elevated far above the surrounding country, and overlooking the long tract of the Severn Sea, is buffeted by every blast.

In fact the highest point is only 356 ft. above sea level. The planting of Weston Woods in the 1820s, and the spread of building, has changed our perceptions from those of the early visitors. To them the village itself looked much like dozens of others in the Mendip region. Near the bottom of the hillside was a small church and its Glebe House; Grove Cottage next door, the seat of the Lord of the Manor; and a huddle of farms and cottages facing the open wastes of the Northmarsh behind the sand dunes. Fields stretched along the hillside, and the skyline was dominated by the ruins of the Celtic or 'Ancient British' fort which had been the home of 'the old men' long ago.

The area was occupied in the New Stone Age and the Bronze Age, and burials and implements from these times have been found on the hill. The Celts, builders of the hillfort, left no written record of themselves. They remain in prehistory, and their culture must be reconstructed from archaeological evidence.

The fort is one of a chain of defensive sites in Mendip Country, of a type that reached full development in the late Iron Age, in the century or two before the birth of Christ. These forts provide evidence of a well organised and populous society. Even today, when the site is covered by trees and the walls of the fort are heaps of stone, a walk around the site reveals

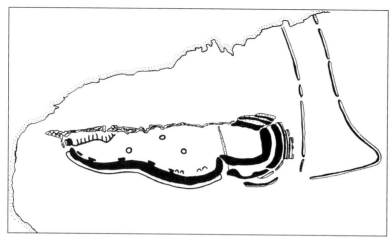

1 A plan of Worlebury hill-fort, based on Dymond. The fort is at the seaward end of the hill, now hidden from the town below by Weston Woods. On its northern side are cliffs which complete the defensive ring made by the massive walls and ditches.

2 Inside the fort 2,000 years ago, by Raymond Dwerry-house. Some of the hut sites have been revealed by recent clearance.

the scale of the construction and the engineering achievement involved in the work. Worlebury fort encloses more than 10 acres and is the second biggest Iron-Age site on the Mendips: only Dolebury (18 acres) is larger.

The walls were originally proper masonry constructions with rubble infilling. Watch-towers flanked the great wooden gates of the three entrances, and the eastern approaches, on the level hilltop, had deep outer ditches and additional ramparts to deter the enemy. The defenders used the slingshot, and stores of pebbles gathered from the beach below have been found inside the fort.

With its secure position and extensive views, the advantages of such a site for the tribe in the warlike times of the later Iron Age are evident. However, the fully developed fort,

probably built between the third and the first centuries B.C., was an extension of an earlier site. It is probably wrong to see the later fort in purely military terms. Worlebury may also have been a status symbol for the tribe, and the centre of local government, commerce, religion and tribal life. Such forts have been compared to the walled towns and cities of medieval times.

Most of the population of the area lived outside the walls, farming from small scattered sites, grazing animals and cultivating the small fields which could still be traced on the hill 150 years ago. The fort itself has an outer enclosure for animals, to the east of the main ramparts and ditches. Although the Celtic peasants could withdraw to the fort in time of danger, they probably spent most of their lives in the outlying settlements, some of which may have been the precursors of the villages around the hill. Celtic pit burials have been found in Grove Park and Stafford Place. The Celts undoubtedly exploited the marshy lands surrounding Worlebury for fishing and hunting.

Inside the fort one can see numerous pits cut into the rock—storage pits for grain. The tops of the pits were sealed with clay, and considerable quantities of grain could have been kept in these Iron-Age stores, giving a supply of food during winter months or in the event of crop failure or siege. Older pits at Worlebury were later used by the inhabitants as rubbish dumps.

The fort's occupants lived in round huts, made of wooden uprights and wickerwork covered with mud or clay. These probably had thatched roofs and a central hearth from which the smoke escaped through a hole at the apex of the roof. Circular remains were noted by early 19th-century visitors, and recorded on plans. Clearance work supervised by Mr. Chris Richards has enabled the sites of at least three hut circles to be identified again, and indeed a number of other possible circles, not shown on earlier plans, have also been found.

North Somerset and South Gloucestershire was the territory of the Dobunni tribe in the later Iron Age. The Celts of this time were increasingly involved in trade with the continent, and therefore to some degree in touch with the Roman Empire, for some time before the Roman invasion of Britain in the first century A.D. It is evident from finds of jewellery and pottery that the Celtic culture was one in which taste had achieved high standards and ornament and refinement were

prized in everyday life. Celtic society had become genuinely civilised in many ways, and the natives of this country were far from being the uncouth savages they were once thought to be.

The Roman invasion came in A.D. 43 and it is thought that the conquest of this part of Britain was complete six years later. (The discovery within Worlebury of several skulls, one with seven sword cuts, once prompted speculation that the site was taken by the invaders in bloody battle, but it is equally likely that the grisly remains date from a time of inter-tribal warfare among the native population.) The Roman presence was quickly established and consolidated in North Somerset after the invasion. The lead mines at Charterhouse, originally run by the military, were a major industrial site, and much of the lead was exported to the continent. Charterhouse lead has been identified at Pompeii. In addition it was probably used at Bath, and in the numerous villas (or Romanised

3   The harbour at Uphill, where the Pill flows towards the River Axe, one of Somerset's major waterways.

farms) which began to dot the neighbourhood. The nearest site of a villa to Worlebury which we know of is at Locking, close to the RAF camp; the villa here was quite a large one. There was a Romano-British temple on Brean Down, across the Axe mouth, built in the middle of the fourth century. It has often been maintained that the port of Uphill, at the southern end of Weston Bay by the Axe, was used to export Mendip lead, and that a Roman road led along the hills to Uphill from Charterhouse, but we cannot be certain of this. Most roads are very ancient and date at least from Celtic times, and simply continued in use during the Roman occupation; but there is no evidence of a Roman road to Uphill in the sense in which this is normally understood. The existence of other routes for the movement of lead from Charterhouse has been demonstrated rather more surely, but no doubt Uphill, at the mouth of an important waterway and offering safe anchorage by high ground, did see much trade during Roman times as it did in other ages.

In Weston the evidence from this period is scanty, but it is enough to demonstrate continuing occupation. Roman pottery was found when the foundations of the College were excavated in the 1960s, together with coins and beads, and there have been other finds in this vicinity between Lower Church Road, Knightstone, and Royal Crescent. The native population continued to occupy the old settlements and farm the same fields on Worle Hill under Roman rule, even though the fort was abandoned.

The Roman occupation seems to have collapsed finally in the early years of the fifth century. There is no evidence that the fort at Worlebury was reoccupied by the native population, although this is known to have happened elsewhere. Nevertheless, the period between about A.D. 400 and 700 almost certainly saw a reversion to Celtic ways as Roman influence faded. In the sixth and seventh centuries Celtic Christian missionaries are thought to have been active along the coastal region of the county. Tradition has it that St Congar founded a monastery at Congresbury. Perhaps there was a St Kew at Kewstoke. The church of St Bridget at Brean has been held to have a Celtic dedication. And of course throughout the Dark Ages the ancient Christian centre of Glastonbury was a beacon of religious life and learning.

The Saxons did not occupy Somerset until well into the seventh century, the Battle of Peonnan in 658 being the crucial breakthrough. With them we enter a time of greater documentation and feel ourselves in a more familiar landscape, not least because so many of our place-names are of Saxon origin. Weston itself is one such—it is the west tun (tun = place, farmstead, or estate). But a Saxon place-name does not prove that a settlement was founded in Saxon times. Saxon names often replaced the older Celtic names of long established settlements, as the native Celtic population was gradually absorbed into Saxon society.

With Weston one is bound to ask the question 'west of what?' Other directional names around Worle Hill—such as Norton, the north tun, and Milton, the middle tun—seem to imply the existence of a central predominant settlement. Nicholas Corcos has suggested that Worle is the most obvious candidate. It was certainly the most important of the villages in later times; Domesday Book of 1086 shows it as by far the richest. Perhaps we see here traces of an older system under which the whole of the area was originally one unit, including the tuns or dispersed farmsteads that gradually developed into more independent settlements.

By the time of Domesday Book, 20 years after the Norman Conquest, this process may have been well advanced, although Weston is not named as a separate manor. It is thought to have formed part of the manor of 'Aisecombe' or Ashcombe, which survived as a small hamlet to the east of Weston until 19th-century development spread out towards it.

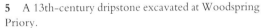
4   Woodspring Priory, 1828.

5   A 13th-century dripstone excavated at Woodspring Priory.

Domesday Book records the names of the other manors whose names we can still recognise: Opopille or Uphill at the south end of the bay; Chiewestok or Kewstoke; Middletone or Milton, which remained linked to Kewstoke, although on the other side of the hill; and Worle, where a small 'motte and bailey' fort at Castle Batch was built in Norman times. There was also the manor of Worspring, or Woodspring, at Middle Hope to the north of Sand Bay, and it may be that there was a settlement here which disappeared after the foundation of Woodspring Priory at the beginning of the 13th century. The Priory ruins still stand, the last monastic ruins of Mendip, and the site is now owned by the Landmark Trust. At some point Weston became a separate manor from Ashcombe, and it is recorded in the time of Henry III that the two manors were both held by the Arthur family of Clapton, near Portishead.

It is only in these centuries after Domesday Book that we find clear evidence of the existence of Weston as a village. Documents of 1226 refer to the Church of St John at Weston, which is to pay 100 pounds of wax annually to the Cathedral at Wells. And it is in medieval church records that we find first the version of the name which has stuck, Weston-super-Mare. This is not a Victorian invention, as is sometimes thought, but the coinage of a medieval cleric writing on the eve of the Black Death in 1348, seeking, we imagine, to distinguish the village from the many other Westons in Somerset. 'Super Mare' is simply Latin for 'on (or above) the sea'. The Registers of the Dean and Chapter of Wells reveal other *ad hoc* ways of identifying the village which failed to catch on: 'Weston-prope-Worle' in 1233, 'Weston-juxta-Worle' in 1311, 'Weston-juxta-Mare', 'Weston-upon-More'. The Norman church appears to have been modified, but not substantially rebuilt, judging by drawings which show it before the rebuilding of 1824. During this rebuilding, Norman details were discovered—a simple round-headed window and some gargoyles—and they can be examined in the Museum.

So how old is Weston? While documentary evidence takes us back only to the early 13th century, it is impossible not to believe that the thread of continuity stretches back much farther. The document of 1226 concerns an existing church. Most Norman churches were re-buildings of Saxon wooden churches, and very few were entirely new foundations. We note that St John's was a parish church by 1226, indicating the existence of an established community (there never seems to have been a church at Ashcombe, which had perhaps been more significant and given its name to the manor at some time before Domesday Book). Weston almost certainly existed as a distinctive settlement and perhaps even a parish, during late Saxon times before the Norman conquest.

6 The Church of St John the Baptist, Weston-super-Mare, before the rebuilding of 1824. It was typical of the churches in the poorer villages of the district, having received some modifications during the late Middle Ages but never having been substantially enlarged.

7 A Norman window arch from St John's Church, now in Weston Museum.

8 The shaft of the medieval churchyard cross outside the south wall of the present church. A carving set in one of the walls outside the tower may be the missing head.

To the east of Grove Park, which we know was the home of the Lord of the Manor in later times, lay the Worthy, shown on early 19th-century maps; the name survives in Worthy Lane (now Market Lane) and Worthy Place. 'Worthy' or 'worth' is one of the most common Saxon place-names and means basically 'enclosure'. It often indicates the approximate site of an Anglo-Saxon farmstead. Another such element found in field names is 'hay' or 'hays' (fence, enclosure), which we find in Blakehay, the name of the field between High Street and Wadham Street immediately to the south of Grove Park ('blake' = black, usually explained in this context as referring to areas of particularly dark soil arising from long periods of cultivation). A Saxon coin was found in Worthy Place. The proximity of the manorial house and the church pinpoint this neighbourhood as the focus of Saxon settlement.

Moreover, the cluster of Romano-British finds is only yards from St John's Church and Grove Park. Historians and archaeologists now tend to stress the continuity between Saxon, Romano-British, and Celtic occupation of sites, for of course throughout the political and military upheavals of recorded history farming and everyday life among the ordinary people subsisted. It is, after all, primarily the logic of the landscape itself which determines human occupation and exploitation, and this logic did not significantly change over the centuries. The deeper soil of the hillside remained the best place to grow crops; the sheltered 'coombes' such as Grove Park remained the ideal sites for farmsteads; and the water supply remained where the springs gushed out of the limestone hill near its base. When we trace the village seen by the first visitors we are also tracing the outlines of a centuries-old pattern of settlement. The early 19th-century maps of the village, drawn when resort development was just gathering pace, show us something of this ancient logic of the landscape.

9   Weston-super-Mare before the parliamentary enclosure settlement.

The village appears to have had two open fields since medieval times, the East Field and the West Field. The former lay beyond the Worthy and above the Bristol Road. The latter covered the area we know as The Shrubbery and beyond. Early 19th-century maps show the remains of these medieval common fields clearly, although by that time they had been reduced by various piecemeal divisions and enclosures. The largest of these is shown as the West Tining or Tyning (the word actually means 'enclosure'). As with other villages along the Mendips, we can see how the fields pushed up the slope to a point where the soil became too shallow to be useful. The open hilltop above was used for grazing animals. This ancient boundary between the fields and the open hilltop was preserved by the parliamentary enclosure settlement of 1815 and is the line we know today as South Road and Cecil Road.

Most of the buildings in the village were set back from the shore and straggled down 'The Street' and onto the moor. The Street is our High Street, while Watersill Road is our Regent Street and Locking Road. At the south end of The Street was what looks like an earlier enclosure from the moor, called 'Wallclose', presumably the origin of our Walliscote Road. Meadow Lane is obviously the start of our Meadow Street, although it only went as far as our Orchard Place. West Lane is our West Street. Dark Lane or Grove Lane wound up the hill beside Grove Park to become what is now Queen's Road.

A small stream ran down the hillside from a spring where Coombe Road is now. On reaching The Street near its north end and Grove Park, the stream turned south to run along the east side of The Street, before turning east to run inland and join the system of rhynes or man-made drainage ditches (pronounced 'reens') that all eventually drain to the Uphill Pill and the River Axe. However, one is bound to speculate that this stream may have originally pursued a more direct route to the sea along West Lane. Two paths ran from the beach here, as if either side of the stream's former course. Whether the old course became blocked naturally or deliberately is an interesting speculation.

The village was at the north end of the bay, and this is the point where high tides threaten the land most. The area of the church and Grove Park is above flood levels, but most of the village was often in danger. Sea walls were maintained by the parishioners from medieval times; obligations to maintain sections of the walls were among the duties involved in local forms of land tenure. From time to time, however, the sea breached the defences, usually when high tides were driven by a strong west wind.

The commoners' rights naturally included the grazing of animals, both on the hilltop and on the moor, although the land belonged to the Lord of the Manor. At certain times of the year the Steward of the Manor had all the beasts and horses driven off the moor to one spot, at the same time assembling their owners. Those who had pasture rights would swear an oath claiming the right, while trespassers were fined. A document of July 1801, recording this ancient custom and entitled 'The usual Rules for driving Weston Moor', says:

> To go to the mark on Uphill Green towards Mrs Kniftings for every person to swear to his stock if required, and for every poor person of the Parish of Weston to pay 10s. if not a common, and all other trespassers at the option of Mr. Pigott or the Parishioners the whole of the stock to be driven on Ashcombe Batch, and the money left after all expenses is paid to be laid out in necessary articles in the parish.

Such manorial customs, adapted to local circumstances, obtained in most villages before parliamentary enclosure, and were survivals from medieval times. They enshrined the balance of rights and duties between the Lord of the Manor and the villagers. Commoners claimed their rights through holding an 'auster' tenement: the word 'auster', commonly used in Somerset, is derived from the Latin 'austrum' (a tenement held in villeinage of the Lord), but was often thought to mean 'ancient'. The word itself was sometimes corrupted and Westonians used to boast that they held an 'oyster' tenement.

At Weston the rights of the austers covered fishing as well as farming, for this was an important part of the local economy. The Severn Estuary offered better fishing than it does today. Salmon were regularly caught, and local tradition required the first salmon of the season to be offered to the Lord of the Manor. Sprats were landed in large quantities. Most local fishing was done with nets, not from boats. The nets were stretched between stakes driven into the bed at low tide. Fishing rights concerned the use of the stakes or 'stalls' at the traditional fisheries at Anchor Head and Birnbeck (where stakes can still be seen along

10   Looking north and east from the site of the Sovereign Centre, 1815.

the natural shingle causeway that connects the island with the mainland). The fish were caught in the submerged nets at high tide, when the currents ran strongly along the headland, and were held as the tide ebbed. Unfortunately, the gulls often got to the exposed catch before the fisherman, so 'gull yellers' were employed to bellow at the birds to frighten them off. One famous gull yeller is said to have been audible as far inland as Congresbury with a following wind.

Fish were an important source of protein in medieval times and later, especially in days when meat was more of a luxury than it is now. Much of the catch was taken to market inland. Fishing rights were therefore valuable, and jealously guarded, as we see from the incomplete record of a dispute of 1492 between John Payne and the Arthur family of Clapton Court, Lords of the Manor of Weston at that time. Payne accused John Arthur of forcibly and illegally fishing in his fishery at Anchor

Head and stated that Arthur's men 'by force of arms namely with sticks and knives fished in the several (i.e. private) fishery ... and took and carried away thence fish namely 100 horse loads of fish called Barons 400 fish called tubbelyns 300 haddocks and 200 whitynges and inflicted other enormities'. He claimed that he had sustained damage to the amount of £26, a large sum in those days. We do not know how the case ended.

Fishing rights were enjoyed by villagers from Worle and Kewstoke, many of whom walked to and from the fisheries every day. The path along the top of Worle Hill, which emerges opposite Birnbeck, is known as the Fishermen's Path. At one point along its length, about 200 yards west of the reservoir, is Picwinner Cairn, a heap of stones on which local fishermen on their way to the shore would throw a stone for luck, repeating this couplet:

Picwinner, Picwinner
Give me a good dinner

11 The fishery at Birnbeck Island. The line of nets on the right follows the shingle causeway which is uncovered at low tide.

Perhaps the cairn was originally an ancient tumulus, or a Saxon boundary mark.

Not many villagers could afford boats. The boat-building trade in this area seems to have been carried on partly for the benefit of leading farmers during later centuries; there was a considerable commerce importing sheep and cattle from Wales. The wealthier fishermen who did use boats sailed in Weston 'flatners', shallow-bottomed craft that were suited to fishing in the bay. Knightstone Island was the local anchorage; like Birnbeck it was reached by a pebble causeway, over which boats could sail at high tide.

The local fishermen had another trade in the 18th and early 19th centuries. Smuggling flourished along these quiet shores, in a period when the import duties on luxury goods were

12   Weston fishermen of the 19th century.

13 The Church of St Nicholas on the hill at Uphill, now partly ruined, contains Norman work. It was a navigation point for sailors. St Nicholas is the patron saint of mariners.

high. Brandy, tobacco, lace and other goods were run ashore at night and hidden until they could be safely moved away, perhaps to be sold to the local squirearchy and aristocrats and rich merchants of Bristol or Bath. The sand dunes or 'tots' at the end of Watersill Road (Regent Street) were said to have been one favourite hiding place for contraband cargo. The excisemen patrolled the coast, usually in vain, for the villagers signalled with lights to waiting boats in the Channel to indicate safe landing places. The area of Prince Consort Gardens, above Birnbeck, was formerly called Flagstaff Hill after the Flagstaff used by the coastguards to signal to the revenue cutter when dirty work was suspected, so that there were two rival systems of communication at work simultaneously. Early Victorian visitors to the resort could still benefit from the thrills and the rewards of local smuggling. In 1845 the *Weston Gazette* reported that 240 barrels of contraband spirits had been landed at St Thomas's Head near Woodspring Priory, and in the following year there was a sale of contraband and condemned merchandise at the Victoria Concert Room. Smuggling declined after the 1840s, once Free Trade reforms had lifted many of the import duties on luxury goods.

Early 19th-century visitors could also see another local industry still in operation—mining on the hillside. The east end of the hill had achieved national importance as a source of calamine, a zinc ore, in the 16th century. It was thought that the ore was discovered in 1566 by German prospectors on land belonging to Sir Henry Wallop, but Nicholas Corcos has discovered evidence that mining was taking place on the hill much earlier in the century and possibly under the aegis of Woodspring Priory. In Elizabethan times, however, the mining rights were leased to the new Society of Mineral and Battery Works, which 'set Tenne or Twelve persons straungers and Englishe on worke to moyne and search for Calamine, which the Countrymen ther do reporte, and gott 20: or 30: tonnes of the said stone'. The ore was found in veins up to three feet thick and the 'gruffy ground' created by lead and calamine mining, still covers areas of the hill, chiefly above Milton and near the fort. Calamine was required to blend with copper in order to produce brass, an alloy increasingly in demand in 16th-century England

for both military and industrial purposes. The Society was granted rights to mine calamine and manufacture brass and brass wire by new methods in 1565, these skills having been learnt in Germany, which was then the acknowledged centre of European metal working.

The company thought of establishing a brass foundry at Bristol, but eventually began work at Tintern on the River Wye, where calamine from Worle Hill was taken by boat. The production of brass seems to have been still experimental and did not proceed well. In 1582 the company leased its rights to four partners who opened a new brass mill in Middlesex: 'the oar, or earth … is brought out of Somersetshire from Mendip Hills, the most from Worley Hill'. Other Mendip mines were developed. Broadfield Down above Wrington was a major source in the 17th century and deposits on the main Mendip range began to be worked at the same time. But the Worle Hill mines seem to have worked into the 19th century, at least inter-mittently, and John Rutter speaks of them as if they were still in operation in 1829. In addition, lead was mined near Christchurch until 1845, and yellow ochre in the Hazeldene Road area until the 1920s.

Chapter Two

The Young Resort

IN THE 18TH CENTURY, when the seaside came into fashion, most resorts were regional in their appeal. Dr. Bryan Brown has pointed out that Bristol and Bath, with their large concentration of the rich and leisured classes, formed the biggest potential body of seaside visitors outside London. However, Bristol was a conservative city and seems to have been late in adopting the seaside habit. Difficulties in travelling weighed against Bristol and Bath establishing a significant connection with South Coast resorts such as Weymouth or Lyme Regis, although attempts were made to develop such a link, and the way remained open for the upper classes from England's second city and from the Queen of the Spas to discover the local coastline of the Severn Estuary.

Weston appears to have come to the notice of outside visitors first through the network of the North Somerset squirearchy. The Manor of Weston had belonged to the Pigott family since 1696. The Pigotts owned numerous manors between Weston and Bristol, and their main seat was at Brockley. They intermarried with the Smyths of Ashton Court, becoming the Smyth Pigotts in the early 19th century. They were an influential family. Family portraits were painted by Gainsborough in Bath. The family appears to have taken a fresh interest in its Weston property during the time of John Pigott (1741-1816), and the second brother, the Rev. Wadham Pigott, was curate-in-charge of the parish by 1790. Wadham was resident in the village and became in effect acting squire, perhaps because of his brother's absences abroad.

During the 1770s or 1780s Grove Cottage or Grove House was modernised, and in 1783 the neighbouring Glebe House was similarly improved. No doubt Wadham Pigott entertained guests in Weston, and before long the Glebe House was being let to staying visitors. The village appealed to members of a social group alert to new fashions and tastes who were wealthy enough to follow their inclinations. One of the first recorded visitors was Hannah More, the well-known writer, philanthropist, and educational reformer, who had

14 The Rev. Wadham Pigott, painted by Thomas Gainsborough in Bath, *c.*1773.

15

15 *Above*. 'Mr Pigot's cottage near the Bristol Channel, Somerset', *c*.1780.

16 *Left*. Grove House, *c*.1828, after the first of the Pigotts' improvements.

17 *Below*. Grove House, *c*.1850, after its enlargement by John Hugh Smyth Pigott.

made her home at Barley Wood, Wrington. She stayed at Uphill (it is thought at Rose Cottage) for health reasons in 1773, and while here formed the acquaintance of Dr. John Langhorne, classical scholar and Rector of Blagdon, who was staying at Weston. In an article in *The Gentleman's Magazine* in 1805 George Bennett, a solicitor from Rolstone near Banwell and a keen antiquarian, wrote:

> This village is much frequented of late in Summer and Autumn for the benefit of sea air and bathing; several good lodging houses having been lately erected for the reception of company. And the Revd. Mr. Leeves of Wrington has built a charming little cottage on the beach, at which himself and family reside a considerable part of the year.

This confirms that Weston was being frequented some years earlier than has generally been thought, although the number of visitors was probably tiny. It is interesting to learn of lodging houses being purpose-built in the very first years of the century, presumably indicating that visitors had already been arriving in sufficient numbers and over a long enough period to lead the unknown builders to have

confidence that the phenomenon was not a flash in the pan. Leeves' Cottage 'on the beach' is said to have been built in 1791, one imagines at least a year or two after the clergyman's first visit. Part of the building, the Old Thatched Cottage, still stands at the corner of Knightstone Road. Its size and character indicate how much the fashionable taste was for going 'back to nature' in something not too different from the farms and cottages of the villagers. It may have been only a 'pretend' cottage, but how different from the elegant town houses of Georgian Bath!

One is bound to conjecture that both Dr. Langhorne and the Rev. Leeves were in Weston in part because of the presence of the Rev. Wadham Pigott, who, besides being an 'elegant and popular' preacher, was also a friendly and amenable companion. His presence in the coastal village certainly explains the visits of the artist George Cumberland between 1802 and 1806. Cumberland was a friend of his, and stayed at the Glebe House, spending much of his time sketching in the parish; he was a friend of William Blake, and became an influential figure in the Bristol School of artists.

18   Leeves' Cottage, built 'on the beach' about 1791. The right-hand section can still be seen.

The beauty and interest of the scenery was a vital part of Weston's appeal to these early visitors. Although the sea itself was rather muddy, this was a delightful and romantic spot, with its wide shallow beach and curving bay, the headland of Brean Down and the islands of Steep Holm and Flat Holm in the middle distance, and Exmoor and the Welsh coast visible farther off. Worle Hill protected the village nestling on its southern slope. It is again the logic of the landscape, rather than some undiscovered historical evidence, which explains the birth of the resort in the last thirty years of the 19th century. It was one of the most attractive spots along a stretch of generally flat coastline. Once discovered it was a magnet powerful enough to draw visitors on a difficult and uncomfortable journey on unimproved trackways to a small village with virtually no civilised amenities.

Perception of the resort's potential at Weston was one of the factors behind the move to obtain an Act of Parliament for the enclosure of the common lands of the village. Parliamentary enclosure was becoming common among North Somerset parishes by the end of the 18th century, the motive generally being a desire for greater agricultural efficiency on the part of leading landowners. Unlike the earlier piecemeal private enclosures it was comprehensive, and ended the commoners' rights over the open land. In 1808 the Pigott family sold a number of the old auster tenements to Richard Parsley, the family's steward at Weston, and William Cox, a tenant of the Pigotts at Brockley, subject to a perpetual ground rent. These two led the initiative and promoted the application for parliamentary enclosure, using as their local agent the Baker family, solicitors, of Aldwick near Blagdon, who had developed something of a speciality in this work; they in turn worked with a specialist lawyer in London. The appointed Commissioner, James Staples, began his task in 1810, and the apportionment of about a thousand acres of common land was settled in 1815.

As was the normal practice the Commissioner funded the process, which had to be self-financing, by auctioning plots of land. This not only paid for his own expenses, but also paid for road improvements and bridges that were part of the improvements carried out. Mr. Staples thought that Weston would spread south and east over the moor, so he chose for auction a number of plots facing the beach south of Watersill Road (Regent Street), as well as some along Watersill Road itself. In 1810 the sea front here consisted of sand dunes which separated the beach from sandy ground behind. Some of the dunes were of considerable height, similar to those that can still be seen towards Uphill by the Golf Course. Sand drifted continually, and there is record of one dwelling, formerly the home of John Gill, which was eventually demolished by the weight of sand that accumulated over the roof. Four lots were sold in July 1810, at prices ranging between approximately £75 and £150 per acre. Five more lots were sold in August 1811, when Mr. Capell of Ashcombe secured a much larger acreage, involving the whole of the beach frontage from the present *Grand Atlantic Hotel* to the site of Severn Road, for £38 per acre. In February 1812 there was a third auction of 36 acres, including the remainder of the beach frontage to the parish boundary where Moorland Road is now and plots along Watersill Road. The development potential of the land was clearly realised. For example, the details of the 1811 auction state:

> These lands are well calculated for building on, there being excellent Spring water to be found on each Lot at the Depth of Fifteen Feet from the Surface; and the Situation is rendered peculiarly desirable, as no Building can be erected between their Frontage and the Sea.

The land closest to the corner of Watersill Road and the beach became the first to be intensively developed, and St James' Street, Richmond Street, and Carlton Street made an early appearance on the maps of the resort.

19 Notice of the auction of lands during parliamentary enclosure, 1811.

SOMERSETSHIRE.

Weston-super-Mare Inclosure.

Notice is hereby given,

That the COMMISSIONERS appointed for carrying into Effect the Act of Parliament for this Inclosure, will proceed to

Sell (in Fee) by Auction,

At the House of Joseph Leman, known by the Sign of the NEW INN,

Situate in the Parish of WORLE, in the County of Somerset,

On Monday, the 8th Day of July, 1811,

Between the Hours of FOUR and SIX in the Afternoon,

THE UNDER-MENTIONED

LANDS,

Subject to such Conditions as shall be then produced.

Lot 1.—A Piece of LAND, Part of Weston-super-Mare Moor, containing by Admeasurement one Acre and an Half, (near the House of the Rev. Mr. Lewis,) bounded Northward by an intended Road, Southward by Lot 3, Eastward by Lot 2, and Westward by the Sea Beach.

Lot 2.—A Piece of LAND, Part of the said Moor, containing by Admeasurement One Acre and an Half, bounded Northward by the said intended Road, Southward by Lot 3, Eastward by Part of the said Moor, and Westward by Lot 1.

Lot 3.—A Piece of LAND, Part of the said Moor, containing by Admeasurement Two Acres, Three Roods, and Ten Perches, bounded Northward by Lots 1 and 2, Southward by Lot 4, Eastward by the said Moor, and Westward by the Sea Beach.

Lot 4.—A Piece of LAND, Part of the said Moor, containing by Admeasurement Five Acres, bounded Northward by Lot 3, Southward and Eastward by the said Moor, and Westward by the Sea Beach.

These Lands are put in small Lots, and selected for Sale for the Accommodation of Persons inclined to build Houses near the Sea and the Village of Weston-super-Mare.

For viewing the Premises, apply to Mr. RICHARD PARSLEY, of Weston-super-Mare, and for further Particulars and Conditions of Sale, to Mr. JAMES STAPLES, Land-Surveyor, at his Office, No. 7, Queen-square, Bristol, or to Messrs. SAMUEL and JOHN BAKER, Solicitors, Blagdon, near Bristol.

RICHARD BISHOP, Auctioneer.

By Order of the said Commissioners,

S. BAKER, Clerk.

BROWN, Printer, Mirror Office, Small-Street, Bristol.

Those who became truly private land-owners throughout the parish as a result of the 1815 Award were those who had been the important figures under the old system. The Pigott family retained all the top of the hill and the greater part of the hillside. The Capell (or Caple) family of Ashcombe Manor Farm secured land at Ashcombe and some of the grazing land on the moor. And Richard Parsley and William Cox obtained the West Tyning on the hillside and a large tract of land south of the village. This new pattern of land ownership (including smaller awards in the village itself) determined the pattern of the resort's development, but building only proceeded at a gentle pace for some years to come. The immediate benefits to the major landowners were in terms of farming. Parsley himself appears to have pursued a 'belt and braces' policy during his lifetime. His land on the moor

20   The former Gunnings Stores at the top of The Scaurs, Worle. Until the 19th century local villages were largely self-sufficient and this was the nearest shop for the young resort.

became the Whitecross Estate, and he built Whitecross Lodge to the south of Watersill Road and east of the old Wallclose enclosure: the house can still be discovered behind the Victoria Methodist Church.

Despite this caution, however, Parsley and the other moving spirits clearly had their eyes on development. It should be noted that their entrepreneurial activities followed Weston's emergence as a watering place, and were not the cause of it. Their confidence must have seemed borne out by the enclosure itself. Out of all the parliamentary enclosures in North Somerset parishes between 1770 and 1830 the selling price of land was higher at Weston than anywhere else, and the economic cost of the

process itself, expressed as a percentage, one of the lowest.

Parsley and Cox were partners in another major initiative when they joined with James Capell and a Mr. Fry to build the resort's first hotel. It became the *Royal Hotel* in later years, and is in South Parade. We see it today with the extensions and new façade that were added in the 1840s. The part nearest Knightstone Road to the north is the original hotel. James Needham was the first tenant, but was apparently unable to attract enough custom, as the hotel closed and its contents were auctioned in 1811. It reopened in 1814 under the management of Mrs. Fry. The stables were built in 1820, the year after Weston's second hotel, the *Bath*, had opened in the new South Parade; it is now the *Imperial*. The *Plough Hotel* was opened in High Street in 1822, so evidently within the decade following parliamentary enclosure business had considerably increased.

Coaches arriving in Weston had completed a difficult and uncomfortable journey, for the village was still isolated in the early years of the 19th century and none of the 18th-century turnpike roads which formed a network around Bristol came anywhere near it. The usual route from Bristol was down the present A38 to Churchill, then to Banwell and Locking Head, and across the low ridge to Worle. The final stretch involved climbing the hill at Worle and following the Bristol Road along the slope, to descend into Weston at the top of High Street. This route was largely superseded from about 1818 by the route through Congresbury, the present A371. Enclosure of Wick St Lawrence and Puxton (1809 and 1814-16) led to upgrading the rough country lanes and tracks between Congresbury and Worle, and the Congresbury Drainage Act (1819) alleviated the regular flooding along this route. In 1814 a limited coach service between Bristol and Weston began, and became a regular service within a few years.

As well as passengers, goods had to be brought to the resort to supply staying visitors and guests. Weston had no shop—the nearest was at Worle at the top of The Scaurs. This was the retail centre for all the local villages. Beer for the hotel had to be brought to Weston by handcart from the Worle Brewery. A bell would be rung to announce that beer was available! In 1806 Messrs. Stabbins and Hill had begun a carrier service in the summer, using wagons, but this was short lived. However, in 1811 John Harse revived the service with success. By 1818 he was advertising a post-chaise hiring service as well, and other competitors were soon vying with him. The establishment of a communications and transport network, and the removal of Weston's virtual isolation from the wider world (especially during winter) was a major factor in the resort's increasing popularity.

21   The Bath House on Knightstone Island built by Dr. Edward Long Fox.

The Enclosure Award of 1815 opened the way for further building. In 1821 there were said to be 126 houses and in 1829, 250, of which 150 were lodging houses. Prices ranged between two and six guineas per week. South Parade had been built, and there were a number of 'gentleman's residences' that ringed the old village. Isaac Jacobs, a Bristol glass merchant, built Belvedere facing Beach Road, and next door was Sidmouth House (both were replaced by the Bus Station). Claremont Lodge was built near Anchor Head. Devonshire Cottage (now part of the *Bayside Hotel* by Manilla Crescent); Highcliffe Lodge in Highbury Road; Wellington Place; Sea View and Belle View (in High Street opposite the Italian Gardens); Weston Hill Cottage (a short way up the Bristol Road); and Vale Cottage at the bottom of Bristol Road, next to the YMCA, which was its 'twin' and originally looked very similar, were all built in these years.

Weston was 'now a fashionable summer retreat' as the first *Guide* of 1822, published by John Chilcott of Bristol, declared.

These early buildings were fairly small, simple two-storey dwellings, built of rubble with stucco rendering. They fitted well into the pastoral and low-key character of the new resort, which continued to rely on its natural attractions and the virtues of sea bathing. The elderly Mrs. Piozzi, better known as Dr. Johnson's friend Mrs. Thrale, wrote from Weston in 1819:

> The Breezes here are most salubrious; no land nearer than North America, when we look along the Channel: and 'tis said that Sebastian Cabot used to stand where I sit now and meditate his future Discoveries of Newfoundland. Who would be living in Bath now? … We have swarms of Babies here, and some bathe good humouredly enough while others scream and shriek as if they were going to execution …

22 A view south from Knightstone Causeway, 1828.

23 The new parish church, *c.*1850. The nave was rebuilt in 1824, and the chancel in 1837. The Glebe House is between the church and Grove House.

Going into the sea was still a frightening experience for many adults too, and attendants, such as the redoubtable Betty Mugglesworth, were on hand to help the nervous and chase away any men spying on the ladies. Canvas awnings were erected at the original ladies bathing place at Anchor Head. When the Hotel opened it boasted the first bathing machine in the village: a changing room on wheels, drawn by a horse into the water, where the modest bather descended steps into the waves. Machines multiplied along the main bay, and continued in use until the beginning of the 20th century.

Sea bathing was only one of a range of treatments at Weston which, soon after the Enclosure Award, began to be recommended by doctors at Bath and elsewhere. Complex medical regimens were prescribed, including the drinking of sea water. Several baths were established in the resort, the foremost being on Knightstone Island. A bath house and pool were opened here in 1822 by Mr. Howe of Bristol, and rented by Benjamin Atwell. The Guide of 1822 made much of the treatments available:

> The bathing establishment consists of a spacious open air swimming bath, plunging and warm baths, either medicated with sulphur, iodine, chlorine or otherwise. The necessary apparatus is also provided for the administration of the douche, and the super-intendent has been instructed in the process of shampooing.

The next owner, the Rev. Thomas Pruen, built a low causeway to the island in place of the shingle path, as well as an open-air pool fed by the tide. A few years later Dr. Edward Long Fox, an influential physician from Brislington near Bristol, spent £20,000 on new facilities. Lodging houses for patients taking 'the cure' were built on the island, and a new bath house in 1832, which can still be seen. There were other baths in Weston, such as Mrs. Gill's in Somerset Place, though these were less elaborate.

Mr. Pruen had built a low pier at Knightstone, the traditional anchorage for local fishermen, some of whom were starting to offer their boats for pleasure trips. The 1822 Guide mentions only two pleasure boats, but in 1829 John Rutter's *Westonian Guide* indicates that the number has grown.

> The Weston pleasure and fishing boats are well built and of a good class. They are accounted to be good sea boats of a sufficient size comfortably to accommodate a consider-able number of persons, but mostly without a deck. They are manned by careful and experienced boatmen, who are remarkably civil and attentive and who generally charge 10s 6d for a day's sail, for a party, or 1s for each.

Steamers began to call occasionally at Weston. Bell's *Comet*, the first commercially viable steam packet in European waters, was built in 1812, and steamers made their appear-ance early in the Bristol Channel because of the importance of the Port of Bristol. The *Duke of Argyle*, built at Port Glasgow the year before, was the first to ply the open waters of the region in 1815, and regular packet services in the Bristol and St George's Channels were begun in 1821. Three years later the *Lady Rodney* was the first locally owned packet to run excursions, from Bristol to Flat Holm and Barry Island, and the following year Weston was included in the itinerary. Trips around the Holms were very popular, but the steamer boom did not begin until the 1840s, when the railways were established.

In 1824, after three years of discussion, the old Church of St John was rebuilt. It had been in a poor state for some years. The old chancel remained for some years after 1824, but a new nave and improved tower changed the church into a place of worship deemed more fitting and commodious for the resort's fashionable visitors. A gift of £1,000 from Wadham Pigott made the work possible—one of his last charitable acts before his death. The new squire, John Hugh Smyth Pigott, perse-vered with the planting of the hillside as a game reserve in the 1820s, thus creating Weston Woods, which were to mature into a fine

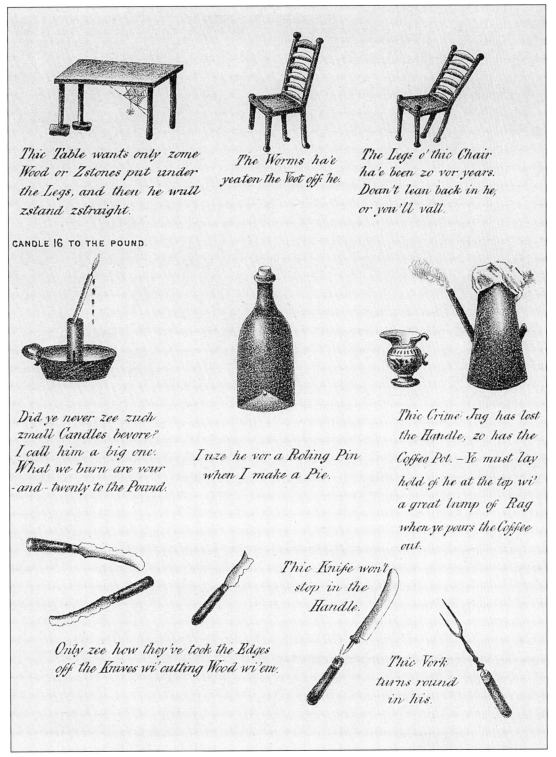

24 Charlotte Wilson's version of the local dialect and her drawings of some farmhouse utensils, 1826.

25 Charlotte Wilson's drawing of The Old Farmhouse, 1826. It stood near Meadow Lane, close to the present Orchard Place.

backdrop for the Victorian town. The woods were thrown open to the public in the 1850s. John Hugh also enlarged Grove House considerably, both to accommodate his own family (he had 10 children) and numerous guests.

By the end of the 1820s there was a low wall and gravelled promenade from Knightstone to Regent Street. Weston was a mixture of town and village, both in terms of physical changes and of attitudes. The encounters between genteel visitors from the polite world and villagers who had grown up in a remote and isolated part of North Somerset could give rise to amusement and disgust—on both sides. This is well caught by Charlotte

Wilson in her account of a visit made from Bath, on medical advice, in 1826. There were no proper lodgings to be had, so she stayed with Farmer King and his family in the old farmhouse in Meadow Lane. The family had sent their best furniture to a new lodging house they had built elsewhere in the village. Charlotte Wilson's narrative is meant to be amusing, but it also captures the 'culture shock' of the local farming family and the fashionable London visitor who likes sketching the local scenery. Her sketches and renderings of the local dialect are a useful record, and a valuable corrective to the inevitable image-building of the early guidebooks.

Chapter Three

Building Victorian Weston

ESTON WAS ONE of the first seaside resorts to enjoy a rail connection and thus became accessible to visitors from farther afield. Isambard Kingdom Brunel stayed at Swiss Villa, a detached mansion in large grounds, which stood where Trevelyan Road is today, while this section of the Bristol and Exeter line was being constructed across the Northmarsh in 1841. It is said that the original proposal to bring the main line closer to the town was opposed by leading local landowners.

The main line passed Weston by, and a branch line was built from 'Wessun Junction' to the first station, which stood where the Floral Clock is now in Regent Street. Winterstoke Road perpetuates the course of the branch line, along which, in the early years, carriages were drawn by horses. The branch line acquired its own steam engine to replace the horses in 1851. The *Railway Hotel* (now *Jack Stamps Beer House*) was immediately to the west of the station.

26   The first railway station, designed by Brunel, which was on the site of the Floral Clock.

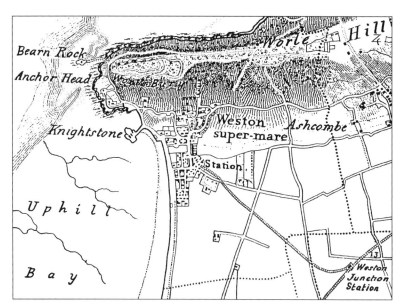

27 A map of Weston in the 1840s showing the branch line of 1841.

Weston's population when the railway arrived was about 2,000 and building had not spread far beyond the area of the old village, as the 1838 Tithe Map reveals. The area of the Beach Road plots had been consolidated, and there was building activity by the beach near Leeves' Cottage. Victoria Buildings, as the name suggests, were new, and the two southerly houses of the seven in the terrace still reveal the character of the originals: simple, small, two-storey properties in the Georgian tradition, with rendered walls, the roofs hidden by parapets, relying upon proportion for their pleasing effect. In West Lane itself, on the other side of Leeves' Cottage, Henry Davies was building the two Beachfield Villas, still to be seen with later additions. These two strike us as modest (apart from the porticoes), but it is recorded that Davies was asked by the Rector of Weston, from whom he had acquired this portion of the glebe land, who he imagined would possibly wish to stay in such spacious premises. Yet within a few years of the railway's arrival Davies was building much grander properties. He was a solicitor, who became Clerk to the new Board of Commissioners in 1842, and was a leading figure among the new generation of entrepreneurs.

Davies pioneered a more ambitious conception of building which was to give Weston some of its most impressive domestic architecture during the following quarter of a century (although building of more modest houses still continued after 1841, as at Albert Buildings 1843, or Wadham Street, begun 1846). He initially concentrated his activity in the area between Victoria Buildings and Lower Church Road. Royal Crescent was begun in 1847, with giant arches in the Roman style. Facing it across ornamental gardens was Greenfield Place, while in Lower Church Road itself, on former glebe land, was Oriel Terrace, originally known as East Terrace. South Terrace, round the corner, repeats the style on a smaller scale. Within a few years Davies had, by the early 1850s, set a new standard of building for the resort. It was not merely that his crescent and terraces were faced with Bath stone, brought by the new railway; these new buildings, as the name of Royal Crescent signals, looked to the architectural traditions of Bath. They are single designs echoing the grandeur of palaces, within which the individual houses defer to the whole.

On the death of Richard Parsley in 1846, Henry Davies and Joseph Whereat, a stationer,

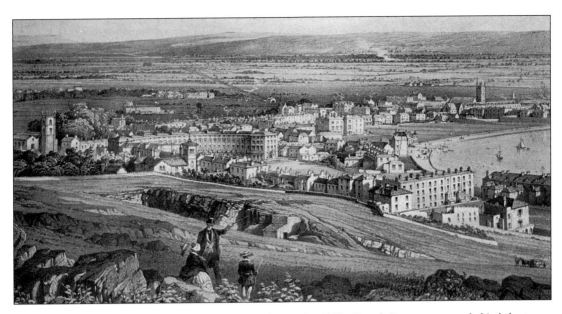

28 The view from the southern rampart of the hillfort in the 1850s. Royal Crescent appears behind the tower of the Villa Rosa. In the foreground is one of the small quarries opened on the hillside, with its own lime kiln.

29 Royal Crescent, built by Henry Davies.

30 Royal Terrace with the *Royal Hotel* on the right, in the 1860s, seen across the Hotel Field which later became the Winter Gardens.

31 Atlantic Terrace and Holy Trinity Church in the 1860s.

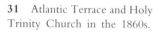

bookseller, newspaper publisher and proprietor of the Assembly Rooms, acquired the Whitecross Estate stretching across the moor to Uphill. In 1855 they began the biggest 'set piece' development in the Bath tradition yet seen in the resort: Ellenborough Crescent, looking across the length of Ellenborough Park to the sea. The new prestige development was named after Lord Ellenborough, former Governor General of India and First Lord of the Admiralty, whose brother, Archdeacon Law, was Rector of Weston. Others adopted this bold approach. The twin halves of Manilla Crescent, facing Glentworth Bay, were built in 1851, and the tradition continued into the next decade with Claremont Crescent, which replaced Claremont Lodge above Anchor Head,

and the two Atlantic Terraces, an audacious concept flanking Holy Trinity Church.

These terraces or crescents indicate a new-found confidence in the resort, which was beginning to benefit through the railway link from the high noon of Victorian prosperity. Wealth, and with it leisure habits, was more widely spread, reaching down the social scale to the professional, trading and manufacturing classes who formed the upper middle class. Thus the resort reflected indirectly Britain's early lead in industrial production and export. Census returns show that many occupants of the new buildings were 'fund holders' living off private incomes and investments. The railway meant that businessmen could live at Weston without being cut off from their offices or factories.

Joseph Whereat observed in the *Weston Gazette* in 1845:

> Weston-super-Mare is found to be just at the most convenient distance from Bristol and Bath, in that gentlemen can easily bring their families hither, and come and return by early and late trains without interruption of their normal hours of business.

By 1854 there were seven trains daily to Bristol from Weston. Many clergymen lived in the resort, and another significant group were the retired Army and Navy officers who had served the Empire overseas.

The new buildings displayed a truly urban spirit for the first time, and this in turn lent credibility to Weston's pretensions to becoming a winter resort and a place of all-year-round residence. The resort had attracted a few winter residents in the 1830s, seeking a good climate for convalescence. The 'change of gear' in building is well indicated in the following, from Wood's *Excursionist's Guide* of 1855:

> Seven or eight years ago, the Beach, Park Place, Victoria and Albert Buildings, may be said to have comprised the chief ranges of private dwellings and lodging houses. Since that period, an immense impulse has been given to building enterprise. As if by magic, there have sprung up Oriel Terrace, the Crescent, Greenfield Place, Prince's Buildings, Manilla Crescent and Wellington Terrace fronting the hill; together with an almost equal number of streets and houses of less note in different parts of the town. The splendour of many of the buildings just enumerated strikes with surprise the unsuspecting visitor on returning to it, after an absence of many years.

At the same time a second building type was becoming established, which in the long run was to prove the more significant. This was the villa, which embodied a tradition quite different from that of the terrace or crescent where all the residences formed parts of a larger whole. By contrast the villa was private and separate in its own grounds, and answered better to the Victorian middle-class ideal. The villa was

32   The footbridge in The Shrubbery which linked the grounds of the Villa Rosa across the road leading to the new villas of the Shrubbery Estate.

detached, although even semi-detached houses met the bill almost as well. As the town broke out of its village straitjacket in the years following the railway's arrival, entire new estates of villas were begun, forming new suburbs. The Grove Estate, to the east of the Grove itself, was the first major development on the Smyth Pigott land, begun in the late 1850s. Grove Town above the Boulevard (Southside) was projected in 1860, the year when the Boulevard itself was laid out (influenced, it is said, by the Lord of the Manor's Francophile tastes). This major new avenue was aligned on the spire of Christ Church, begun in 1854, itself the focus of the new Montpelier Estate where building began in 1858. The area around Ellenborough Park was developed with large villas from the 1850s onwards. On the hillside to the west, the grounds of the Villa Rosa (a striking Italianate mansion of the 1830s) were developed as The Shrubbery Estate, and westward again the district around Holy Trinity Church, known as Cliftonville, was begun. The houses above South Road began to be built in the 1860s. The only project of this kind which failed to materialise was the Swiss Villa Estate, to the south of Montpelier; being close to neither the hill nor the sea but only to the new main road and artisans' cottages, it lacked the advantages of setting to compete with the other initiatives.

Setting was important; most of the new estates were, in their early years, separated from the town centre by fields, and they maintained an exclusive air. Their roads were private and sometimes protected by gatekeepers' lodges, which in some cases can still be seen. Each villa had its private garden, soon filled with the shrubs beloved of the Victorians, and several of the estates also had communal gardens for the sole use of the residents (the Shrubbery, Ellenborough Park, Landemann Circus, Eastfield Park). Original plans of these handsome houses reveal a layout calculated for a comfortable lifestyle: not only a lounge, dining room, breakfast room, several bedrooms and 'usual offices', but also a wine cellar, billiard

room, or study. Bay windows gave fine views from the principal rooms, which had high ceilings with plaster decoration, and large imposing fireplaces. The villa was designed for restful, secluded and comfortable retirement in leafy surroundings, solid yet stylish and confident: an emblem of Victorian middle-class values and aspirations.

In these havens of genteel respectability there were no shops of any kind, and, naturally, no public houses. The villas all had servants' quarters, either in the attics, rear wings, or semi-basements, which can still be identified. The Census returns show that most villas had at least two living-in servants, drawn in the main from the surrounding villages. Cooking and heating consumed large quantities of coal, brought in to Knightstone Harbour, and the tall chimney stacks are a prominent feature of these buildings. Goods were delivered by horse or donkey from shops in the town centre. The town had numerous mews from which horses and carriages could be hired when required.

Whereas the terraces and crescents boasted Bath stone façades, Weston's villas soon began to use the better quality carboniferous limestone that was now being produced from the Town Quarry and others in the district. This hard grey stone is actually better suited to withstand the rigours of the coastal climate. However, the softer Bath stone continued to be used around doors and windows, in quoins, corbels, and for decorative ornament, as it could be cut easily.

By the 1860s local limestone and freestone were superseding brick or rubble walls covered with render even in the new working-class dwellings which were filling up spaces on the flat land around the town centre; Palmer Street and Alfred Street are good examples. George Street was begun in the 1870s, largely to provide guest and lodging houses. The National Freehold Land Society began building around Clarendon Road in the late 1860s. There was a degree of continuity, in terms of building materials, throughout the town, and working-

33   The roofscape of Weston villadom: looking over Grove Park Road and Queens Road, towards the Mendips.

34   The roofscape of working-class Weston: looking south down Palmer Street.

35 Architect's drawings of a typical villa built on the
Weston hillside, 1892. Notice the servants' wing and
back stairs, which make the two sections of the house
independent of each other.

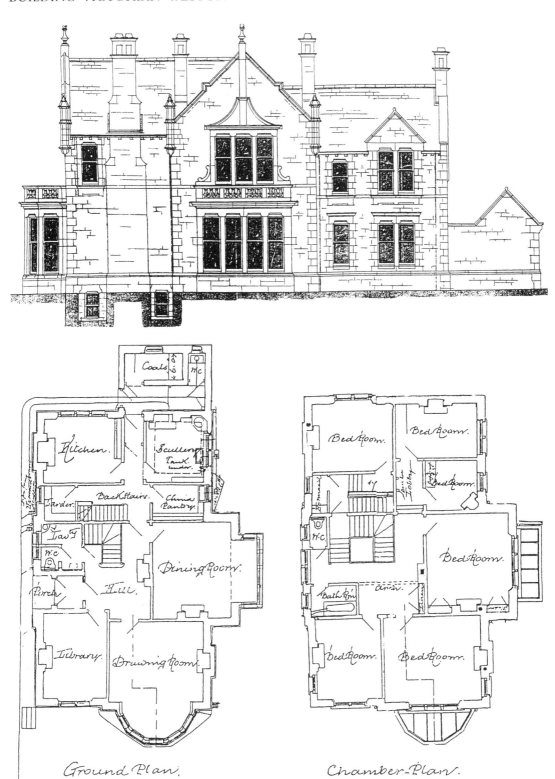

Ground Plan.

Chamber-Plan.

36   A rare view of construction taking place: the left half of Manilla Crescent being built, 1851, with Glentworth on the right.

class houses in Weston were sturdy buildings. The villa itself was capable of adaptation to the needs of lower social groups, and as the century progressed more modest versions of the semi-detached style were built for the lower middle classes. The process reached working-class homes towards the turn of the century, and the style replaced the terraced housing of the older workers' streets. There was a consistency in terms of building materials throughout the town until the First World War.

Estate development was a particular residential form, favoured by many local land-owners as it was in many towns and cities in Victorian England. Large tracts of land were offered for building, and individual plots were sold or leased subject to strict conditions. These controlled not only the layout of the estate but also the size and type of dwelling to be built, the materials to be used, the completion date

and the ultimate price. The system guaranteed that all the houses in an area blended with each other, even though several different builders may have been responsible for them. It also ensured that the 'tone' of the estate was maintained. Land could be released gradually, at a rate dictated by the market. This was the form of development on the land progressively released by the Smyth Pigott family, who used the unusual system of selling plots subject to a perpetual rent charge. A typical rent charge for a hillside property was, and still is, £10 per annum. This system not only brought in capital but also an income after the land was sold and the houses completed. Estate development in this form also enabled the Smyth Pigott family to ensure a degree of town planning and aesthetic control.

From soon after the mid-point of the 19th century effective control of the Smyth Pigott

37 Manilla Crescent, *c.*1890.

38 Manilla Crescent, *c.*1985.

estate at Weston was in the hands of a small network of professional men. The agent was Robert Landemann Jones (after whom Landemann Circus is named) who was born in Barnstaple in 1816. Jones himself ran away to sea when a boy, and apart from a brief period in a solicitor's office he remained on the China coast for 18 years, being commander and part owner of his vessel. He returned to England, married in 1847, and took up farming; some of this period he spent at Blagdon, where he no doubt became acquainted with the Baker family, solicitors to the Smyth Pigott estate. He took over management of their estates about 1860 and recouped their profitability. In 1872 Jones told a dinner of the Master Builders at Weston that the estate had built 250 houses in the preceding 10 years, increasing the rent roll by £2,500 per annum.

The need to secure a regular income for the estate was underlined by the difficulties into which the Lord of the Manor, John Hugh Wadham Smyth Pigott, had run. He seems to have been a difficult character in many ways. It was not merely that he was a lover of Paris who became a convert to Roman Catholicism, endowing the first Roman Catholic church at Weston, St Joseph's; it appears that he also amassed large gambling debts. A trust was established to salvage his affairs. In 1855 there was a mortgage of estate land, including some in Weston, to secure £10,000 and interest. Even the Grove House was let for a while, the family moving to a house overlooking Prince Consort Gardens. Jones was a principal figure in redeeming the family fortunes, but relationships between the squire and his agent were often tempestuous. We read in 1861:

> Rumours have been rife during the week, to the effect that Mr R. L. Jones, the agent to John Hugh Smyth Pigott, Esq. ... had been peremptorily removed from the management of the estates, and that removal had taken place in consequence of certain disclosures, which will in all probability lead to a suit in the Court of Divorce.

Pigott and his wife were the subject of a 'skimmity ride' after his wife, who was much younger than her husband, gave birth to a son in 1860 and there were rumours that the squire was not the child's father. A local rabble paraded past the house above Flagstaff Hill one evening carrying effigies of their luckless victims. The child was Cecil, later Lord of the Manor in his turn, after whom Cecil Road is named.

The naming of roads was itself one of the numerous causes of friction between John Hugh Wadham and the Town Commissioners, who had been established by Act of Parliament as the local government body soon after the coming of the railway. The Board of 18 members had only limited powers at first, but their role grew in line with reforming legislation throughout the Victorian period. The Commissioners tended to include the leading developers and entrepreneurs of the town, whereas John Hugh Wadham was a bastion of the old county ruling class. He was taken to task by the Commissioners in 1870 for putting up name plates in the new roads without their permission. The letter columns in the local press resounded with mutual accusation. One writer described the Lord of the Manor as a 'useless member of the community'. John Hugh Wadham in turn abused the Commissioners 'more than half of them being only colonists and squatters on my manor, and the other half parvenus and upstarts'. Of one particular correspondent he said, 'he is not worthy to clean my servant's boots'. On another occasion the squire was outraged when the Commissioners installed a public seat by the Toll Road to Kewstoke. He had his men pull it up and deposit it outside the Town Hall. These upsets cannot have made the harmonious development of the resort easy during the boom years.

A fashionable watering place in the 19th century was not expected to have any industry. It offered an escape, for those who could afford it, from the grime, pollution, and ugliness that disfigured many of the inland towns and cities. For working people in Weston and the

39 Building a villa on the hillside.

surrounding villages employment prospects were therefore limited to trade and service, as well as work on the farms and market gardens that supplied the fashionable visitors and residents with the necessities of life. Apart from this, Weston was not a working town, and did not become one to any significant extent until well into the 20th century.

The one exception in Victorian Weston was the building industry itself. Census returns reveal a small army of those belonging to the various building trades and their labourers: masons, bricklayers, plasterers, carpenters, painters, plumbers, slaters and tilers. Their work was often seasonal.

Vast quantities of stone were taken from the Town Quarry, which developed from the village gravel pit. The Enclosure Act enshrined the rights of owners of 'old auster or ancient tenements' to take stone for building or the repair of roads. Methods of working changed little over the years. Stone-getters normally worked in small gangs, and each gang was responsible for its own blasting, breaking, and haulage within the quarry. The method of boring for the shot-holes was to 'jump the holes down', working a rod up and down until the hole was about six feet deep. Rows of holes were drilled two or three feet apart, and then filled with charge and a fuse cable. The resulting explosion might lift out between ten and thirty tons of stone.

Mechanisation only made its appearance in the later years of the century. Steam power made drilling and crushing easier but the quarry was still a dangerous place. Its proximity to some of the most prestigious villas in the town was an embarrassment. Blasting sometimes sent stones into the leafy retreats of leading residents, who in 1879 petitioned the Commissioners to enforce tighter controls. At a meeting one of the Commissioners himself produced stone that had come through his window while he was shaving. However, the Commissioners were advised that, as the quarry had been there first, before the houses, there was little that could be done. If the local gentry suffered inconvenience the quarrymen themselves faced constant danger and even death in blasting accidents. For example, in 1886 a quarryman named Edward Vile, who lived in Palmer Street, died after a charge exploded late; he left a widow and two children.

There were many other small quarries along the hillside, some of which now form the gardens of villas built from the stone won

on the site. Towards the end of the century Milton Quarry was developed, and was later given modern bottle kilns for lime burning by Henry Butt, a self-made local businessman. The *Windsor Castle* at Milton was originally called the *Masons' Arms* because its trade was drawn from the local quarrymen.

Stone masons at the top of their trade were able to dress the hard local stone so precisely that in many buildings it was used as ashlar, although more often it was laid random. Some of the 'old-timers' could dress the stone with a sledgehammer ready to go straight into a wall. Their skills were in such demand in the rapidly growing resort that they felt able to strike in 1858, at the height of the first building boom; in April between 100 and 150 masons and their labourers were on strike. The masons, who earned £1 a week, were demanding two shillings a week more and a half-hour a day less work, but the master builders wanted to cut wages by two shillings and keep the same hours. The strike lasted for several weeks and must have been an unprecedented example of organised militancy in the town. An increase of one shilling a week was eventually agreed.

40   A gang on the quarry face.

41   Building the road at Milton Hill.

42   Charles Phillips (1816-94), who expanded the potteries in Locking Road.

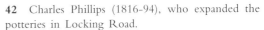

There were numerous lime kilns in the area, such as the one at Uphill near the boatyard. Coal dust and small coal was used to burn stone rubble loaded into the top of the kiln, and the resulting burnt lime was raked out of a smaller opening below; this was used both on the land and in lime mortar. Kilns were kept burning for weeks at a time, being topped up with alternate layers of coal and stone, and the draught controlled by openings in a 'lean-to' built against the side over the lower opening.

Local potteries were major suppliers to the building trade. William Wilcox took over a pottery in Locking Road in 1841, and a second site was in operation a few years later, which was taken over in 1847 by Charles Phillips, an illiterate local man who manufac-tured flower pots as well as bricks and tiles. His products won an honourable mention at the Great Exhibition of 1851, and the venture became the 'Royal Potteries' after winning the contract to supply the royal parks. A wide range of garden urns and other ornamental pieces were developed alongside the more routine articles. By the 1880s, when flower pot production reached 1½ million a year, the potteries were rated the largest single source of production in England.

The clay was generally dug in the autumn, and spread out and left to weather until spring. It was then turned several times and put through a pug-mill and wedged to remove air bubbles. Clay for bricks was mixed with sand to prevent shrinkage and to encourage the bricks to fire all the way through. Brick clay was either cut with wire or pressed into wooden moulds, and the tools were also made of wood, often by the men themselves. The moulds were always slightly larger than the required size of the finished article, to allow for shrinkage during firing. In the kilns, the bricks were stacked around the walls and the flower pots 'nested' in the middle. One can still see many examples of the pottery's tiles and ridge tiles on local houses, their cheerful orange-red colour making a happy contrast with the local stone. The

business was bought by John Matthews in 1871, and was taken over by Conway Warne in 1888. Demand fluctuated with the fortunes of the building industry; at one point the venture was rescued from bankruptcy and re-launched by the Pigott estate, which had a vested interest in the local building market.

By 1900 the old potteries site was worked out. Building had spread out of town to reach its limits, sending up the price of land and making expansion of the site uneconomic. A new site at Langford Road was brought into operation. Brick production boomed for a while, but by the 1930s it was the humble flower pot that was the mainstay of the business. Plastic pots eventually brought it to an end, and the firm went into voluntary liquidation in 1961.

The town had its own sawmills in Meadow Street, and its own iron foundry, which began as Pond's in 1840 but was taken over by Hillman's in 1850 and survived until 1962. The foundry was at the south-east corner of Richmond Street and produced gates, railings,

43   The Locking Road potteries in the 1880s.

44 John Parr with a 48in. pot in the 1890s.

drainpipes and covers, lamp posts and street nameplates, many of which can still be seen. Good communications made the import of some materials relatively easy, the most notable being Welsh slate and Bath stone. The blue or violet tints of roof slates mingled with local pottery tiles to give the hillside town an attractive roofscape, while honey-coloured Bath stone, the prestige building material of the time, came by rail from its source only thirty miles away.

Weston's presiding architectural genius was Hans Fowler Price, who established his practice in Weston at about the same time that Jones took over management of the Pigott estates, and worked closely with him. Price was born in 1835 at Langford near Weston, and was articled to Thomas Denville Barry of Liverpool. He set up practice at 5 High Street

in 1860, living at 5 Victoria Villas, three doors away from Samuel Baker of the family firm of solicitors that acted for the Pigott estates. In 1862 Price married Baker's sister, Jane, and the couple lived for nearly thirty years at 'Tyn-y-Coed' in Hill Road. The Bakers' role in running the manor estate was considerable, and the connection helped Price to become consulting architect for the Pigott developments. He designed scores of villas that filled Jones' new suburbs, varying the basic formula with individual touches and decorative details so that each property had its own character and identity. His role in the team that developed the Pigott land was crucial in setting the tone of the growing watering place.

The railway had opened the way for the building boom, and the town's population

45 Hans Fowler Price, 'the doyen of the architectural profession at Weston'.

46 Weston's three railway stations, and the track layout after the third station and loopline had been built.

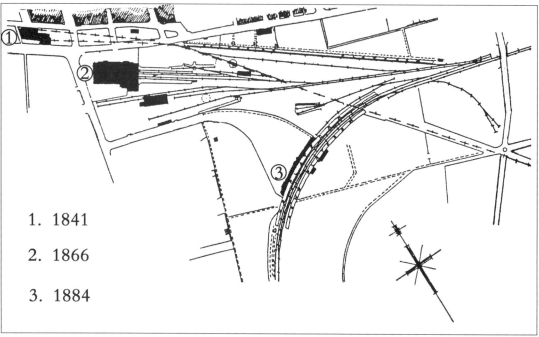

1. 1841

2. 1866

3. 1884

47   Weston Station, 1896.

expanded rapidly. From just over 2,000 in 1841 it doubled to just over 4,000 in 1851 and then doubled again to just over 8,000 in 1861. Thereafter it climbed steadily to reach over 18,000 at the end of the century. It was not long before the original station and branch line were proving inadequate to cope with the increased traffic in and out of the resort. A second station was opened in 1866 on the site now occupied by the Tesco store next to the Odeon. It was much larger, with a long excursion platform and a goods shed. Passengers alighted in front of the Town Hall at the end of Oxford Street, but they had still to travel along the old branch line. In 1875 this was converted to mixed gauge, and the following year the Bristol and Exeter Rail-

way Company was absorbed into the Great Western. In 1878 Brunel's old broad gauge finally disappeared and the branch was standard gauge only. The Great Western was keen to link Weston to the main line by a loop, and work began on the present loopline in 1882. When it was completed two years later Weston's present station was opened, the town's third. Much of the second station survived as the goods station, and there was now an excursion platform nearly a quarter of a mile long, stretching from Alexandra Parade towards the Gas Works. This complex track layout remained in use for nearly eighty years. The goods station closed in 1960, and the excursion platform was demolished in 1967.

Chapter Four

Public Works

HOUSE BUILDING SURGED AHEAD in the years following the railway's arrival, but other developments were also necessary to support the relaxed life style of the new residents and visitors. A basic infrastructure was created using the new technology and engineering skills of the age to provide the often unseen services which the imposing new residences required in order to function. Sometimes enterprising individuals filled a gap; at other times new forms of public organisation emerged to meet local needs. It should be remembered that during this period social and economic change was dominated by a utilitarian ethos which reflected the manufacturing and commercial interests that were rising in the country generally. The new entrepreneurs distrusted public legislation and trusted to the unregulated efforts of individuals to achieve harmonious economic order and well-being.

Shops naturally appeared as housing spread. There had been none in the village, and the first in the young resort was Cornelius Hancock's in The Street, which became High Street, the principal shopping street in the town; its curving line is still a reminder of village days. At first extensions were thrown out over the front gardens of dwelling houses, but increasing rebuilding produced more adequate shop premises, many of which we can see today. By the late 1850s High Street had over forty shops, half the total in the town. High Street was not completely built up because covenants enjoyed by early lodging houses guaranteed

their open views to the beach; hence the Italian Gardens area remained as a field belonging to the *Royal Hotel*, and visitors to the best shops passed allotments and cattle grazing in the heart of town.

Later Victorian shops had ornate fronts, with handsome fascias and ornamental woodwork. Plate glass windows became common, allowing elaborate displays of goods. The design of shopfronts was of a piece with the architecture, embodying quality and reliability. Shops had gas lighting and it was normal for them to stay open until eight or nine o'clock in the evenings.

Regent Street and St James Street were other early shopping streets. At the seafront end of Regent Street was Whereat's Reading Room and Assembly Rooms, an important institution for those with time on their hands and cultural pretensions. The original building of 1826 is now incorporated into the *Beach Hotel* opposite the Grand Pier. Whereat was another important figure who profited from the post-railway boom, the publisher of the town's first newspaper, founded in 1845. New Assembly Rooms were built by a limited company of townspeople in 1858 at the corner of West Street and High Street but were a casualty of bomb damage in the Second World War.

St James Street was considered by some to be as important as High Street in the early years of the town. Rufus Palmer, whose father had come to the town from Lympsham in 1830 and who eventually started a bootmaking

48   The Assembly Rooms were built at the end of Regent Street in 1826 and now form part of the *Beach Hotel*.

49   High Street during the First World War: a queue for margarine.

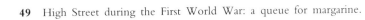

business, described his childhood memories of the street in his autobiography. He was born in 1846, and the family's shop was Number 12. Here Rufus grew up with his six brothers and sisters and his parents, 'not only highly respectable, but pious and Godfearing Persons'.

> In those days plate glass had not been introduced. Our shop front consisted of about a dozen squares of glass, about 24 ins. by 18 ins., enclosing a window-board whereon was displayed a few samples of my father's wares, a pair of top boots—top boots were generally worn in those days by the gentry—various other boots and shoes and a pair or two of worked slippers.

One of young Palmer's best friends was Albert King, whose father kept the *White Lion* public house across the street (the lion is still over the door), and nearby in the street were Johnny Walker's leather and grindery shop, Cole's fishmonger's and fruiterer's business, and Bradbury's Pawnbroking Establishment.

The junction of Regent Street, High Street and Meadow Street had been the site of the village green, a small area now the site of the HSBC. It remained in many respects the hub of community life, recalled in its old name of Gossip Corner. Present Westonians remember it by its later name of Big Lamp Corner, after the gas

50 Regent Street, *c.*1850. The Wesleyan Church is on the left at the corner of St James's Street.

51 High Street, 1861. The spire denotes the Independent Church of 1858, now Woolworths.

52 Weston donkey chair men.

lamp that stood here. This was the scene of New Year celebrations and the place to meet on summer evenings. While the sea front was the place for promenading, Gossip Corner remained the meeting place for local working people. To the south was the first working-class area, now largely redeveloped. To the east was the second area of workers' streets, opening off Meadow Street, built during the 1850s and 1860s. This area survives intact, and one can still explore a district which housed hundreds of working families in simple terraced dwellings, with workshops and small businesses hidden behind. The shops in Meadow Street—still the most important 'local' shopping street—served this tightly knit community.

More prestigious commercial buildings appeared later in the century, and Hans Price designed several, including Magdala Buildings (1869) on the corner opposite the Odeon Cinema, and the richly ornamented terrace on the east side of North High Street; the latter incorporated a new façade for the Market (now the Playhouse), which had originally been out of doors, moved into its first building here in 1827, was rebuilt in 1858, and was redesigned by Price in 1900. The northern part of the town centre attracted many of the superior businesses, and also the banks. There was one at each end of South Terrace: Stuckey's Bank, and a branch of the Wiltshire and Dorset where Lloyds TSB is today. Waterloo Street was

53   The Boulevard, looking east from Waterloo Street.

opened up in 1860 and acquired some hand-some premises connecting the town centre with the Boulevard and including Price's own offices at Number 28.

In 1812 letters had been delivered once a week by a man on a donkey; 10 years later the resort was a penny post from Bristol. A Stamp Office opened in 1844, and the first Post Office was established at 5 Somerset Place, High Street in 1855. In 1875 the Post Office moved to a site next to the *Market House Inn* and now occupied by Threshers; there were stables for the Post Office down Old Post Office Lane. In 1899 a new General Post Office opened overlooking the Hotel Field on the site of the former Veranda House.

As the town grew rapidly in the middle years of the century it drew in traders from far afield. Taking Wadham Street as an example, the 1851 census shows it to have contained a druggist from Devon, a tea dealer from Worcester, a plasterer from Hereford, a brewer from Wiltshire, a dressmaker from Devon, a chairman from North Petherton, a grocer from Butcombe and a tailor from Spaxton.

Weston's Commissioners had only limited scope for action in their early years: street lighting, drainage, paving and 'watching' (organising the watch) were their only powers, and Alfred Street was the eastern limit of their jurisdiction. They could raise a rate, which was set at ninepence in the pound in the first year.

One of the Commissioners' first measures was to organise the widening of High Street, where there had hardly been room for two carriages to pass.

Drainage and sewage constantly exercised the minds of Weston's leaders. It was not simply the practical necessity of catering for a rapidly increasing number of private dwellings that made this an early priority of local government in the town. A watering place was jealous of its reputation as a healthy resort for invalids and hypochondriacs, in an age when conditions were often appalling in inland towns and cities and epidemics were a constant threat. The early town simply took advantage of the system of ditches or rhynes that criss-crossed the moor and found their way into the Uphill Great Rhyne, the Uphill Pill and the Axe; or properties relied upon cess pits. In 1842 the Commissioners accepted a tender from Benjamin Brice for building the first proper sewers in the town. In 1850 there were complaints about the sewage in the Uphill Rhyne, and the following year the Commissioners held a competition for proposals to overcome the nuisance and the inadequacies of the system; a sewer was laid from Milton Road along Ashcombe Road to disinfecting works in Drove Road in 1856.

The fluctuating population of a resort was part of the problem. The sudden arrival of thousands of visitors put an enormous strain on the services and sewage seeped from the open rhynes into wells. Fevers and deaths as a result of pollution were fairly common, especially among the poorer classes. Weston had a healthy reputation, and certainly was healthier than many places, but standards are relative. There was still nervousness about anything that might undermine the salubrious image.

In 1865 Joseph Bazalgette was retained to propose a new drainage scheme. He was the leading authority on the subject: Chief Engineer to the Metropolitan Board of Works and responsible for building London's trunk and outfall sewers and the Thames Embankments.

Bazalgette's system for Weston was swiftly implemented through two contracts: one for a 48-inch brick outfall sewer from the Drove Road works to the River Axe at Uphill; the other for an egg-shaped brick interceptor sewer from Orchard Street to the Drove Road site. This major scheme, involving 5,000 yards of sewers in trenches that were sometimes at a depth of 25 ft., was completed in 18 months and cost £17,000. The ground was difficult to work in, being soft and liable to slip. Frequent additions were made to Bazalgette's system over the remaining years of the century.

In other spheres limited companies stepped in to meet specific needs (often with some of the Commissioners as directors). It was a private company that built the first gasworks in Oxford Street in 1841 (opposite the end of New High Street, formerly known as Gas Lane). As well as the 42 public lamps there were originally 50 private subscribers. The gasworks site was too central to be quite the thing in a fashionable resort, and new works were soon built 'out of town' at Drove Road (1852-6).

The same approach was adopted to the question of water supply. Many houses, of course, had their own wells, and the large-scale Ordnance Survey sheets of the 1880s show that there were also numerous communal wells in the poorer districts. Before tapped water was available more care was taken to avoid waste; in 1850 the public water pumps were padlocked because children had been wasting water. The Waterworks Company, led by Henry Davies, was established in 1852 and built its reservoir on the site of natural springs in Milton Road (at the bottom of Ashcombe Park), with a higher level tank in Lower Bristol Road by the gate lodge of Montpelier. The water was pumped up by steam engine. The quality of the water was said to be very pure but exceedingly hard. During one week in June 1891 the Ashcombe wells supplied over 3½ million gallons. The high-level reservoir in Weston Woods was built in 1865, and the company was purchased by the Commissioners in 1878.

54   The water tower in The Shrubbery, which had its own private water supply before the villas were connected to the waterworks company's system.

55   Athletic meeting of the Volunteer Fire Brigade, 1890, opposite the Hotel Field in High Street.

An unofficial volunteer fire brigade had been formed in 1846, at the behest of local traders. It was sponsored by the Commissioners and had a manual fire appliance. The Brigade was remodelled in 1879, and obtained a steam pump engine in the 1880s, when it had 14 members who met for drill weekly.

The churches and chapels were behind many of the town's philanthropic endeavours. On the whole the Church of England pre-dominated among the well-to-do. The building of new churches came early in the development of the new residential suburbs, although the first, Emmanuel Church in Oxford Street (1847), was a deliberately missionary under-taking directed at the working-class population in that district. It had seating for 625 people. The first pastor was a remarkable man, the Rev. John Hamilton Forsyth, who had been called 'the best B.A. in Cambridge', and who became curate at St John's in 1839 at the age

of twenty-three. He worked tirelessly among the local poor, making friends and holding meetings in cottages and in the open air. He lived just long enough to see the new church opened before he died at the age of thirty-one. Christ Church (begun 1854) provided a focus for the new estate of Montpelier even before most of the villas there were built. In the same way Holy Trinity (1860) was the centrepiece of the Shrubbery and Cliftonville district, and was facetiously known as 'the hat shop' because of the display of wealth and fashion to be seen there every Sunday. All Saints (1898-1902), designed by C.F. Bodley in place of the temporary 'iron church', is one of the most impressive architecturally. St Paul's (1912) at the south end of Walliscote Road was heavily bombed during the Second World War.

A guidebook of 1850 declared: 'the Dissenting interest generally, in Weston, as in most watering places, is rather low, being greatly submerged by the attractive and more powerful influence of the Church'. Nevertheless the places of dissenting worship were more in evidence in the town centre, a telling sign of the resort's social geography. The first Methodist meetings were held in a converted cottage in Wellington Lane, but in 1847 a new Wesleyan Church opened in Regent Street and it was said that 'its Gothic architecture might easily be taken for an episcopal edifice'. In the 1860s this was enlarged to provide seating for 500. The building, on the corner of St James Street, has been converted into a bank. It closed as a church in 1899. The Victoria Methodist Church in Station Road had opened in 1849 because the Regent Street church was too small; it was rebuilt in 1936 after a fire. There is another former Methodist Church to be seen on the Boulevard-Orchard Street corner. The United Methodists had a chapel in Burlington Street which was taken over by the Bible Christians when the congregation moved to a site in Locking Road at the east end of the Plantation; this building later became a motor cycle shop.

An Independent Church was built in High Street in 1830, and before long this too was found to be inadequate. It was rebuilt in 1858. In 1876 the congregation moved to the Boulevard Congregational Church at the east end of Waterloo Street. The High Street building was purchased by Felix Thomas who converted it into an ironmonger's shop; the spire was taken down and incorporated in Banwell Abbey. The shop is now Woolworth's, and one can still see some of the buttresses and windows which betray its origins; the store was extended at the back, and the schoolroom and six cottages were demolished for the enlargement.

A third group to find rapid rebuilding necessary was the Baptists, who opened a church in Wadham Street in 1850. This building was enlarged in 1862 by Hans Price (his earliest known public commission). It is now the Blakehay Arts Centre. Price also designed the Baptist Church in Lower Bristol Road in 1870.

Land for a Friends' Meeting House had been given by Richard Parsley in Oxford Street

56   The Congregational Church in Waterloo Street, built in 1876. It was bombed during World War II and the present building re-uses the Victorian foundations.

57   Christ Church, 1877, during enlargement. It was built in 1855 to serve the Montpelier Estate.

58 The Wadham Street Baptist Church of 1863, where Hans Price re-used the pillars and other details from the building of 1850.

59   The Bristol Road Baptist Church, 1870.

in 1846 (another casualty of bomb damage). As with other Dissenting groups there is some evidence that wealthy Bristol merchants and others supported congregations at Weston. Not all the rich visitors to the resort were members of the established Church, and it was a prudent policy to help meet the needs of all. Roman Catholics were meeting at the *Railway Hotel* in 1853, and five years later they opened St Joseph's, tucked away on a small site on Pigott land in Camp Road. The Cemetery was opened in 1856, well beyond the edge of town along the Bristol Road, with a gate lodge and gothic chapels, one of which survives. The old churchyard of St John's and the new church-yards at Emmanuel and Christ Church were closed for burials, and Holy Trinity, built soon afterwards, has no graveyard. The Cemetery was extended in 1917, taking in the gate lodge of Ashcombe House, a detached mansion built by the Capells of Ashcombe, part of whose grounds formed the new extension.

It is evident that the combined congregations of all these churches added up to many hundreds in the later years of the century, their numbers regularly swelled by seasonal visitors. All had their Sunday Schools and varied social activities, and all made a contribution to the town's welfare. Official provision for the relief of poverty was limited to the Work House, which does not figure much in the town's annals. During its early years as a town Weston still formed part of the Axbridge Union and the Work House was in the old market town. The Weston Work House was built later on the edge of the Hospital site by Baker Street. This was on glebe land belonging to Christ Church, which originated many efforts to help poorer townspeople with 'outdoor relief'. There was a Soup Kitchen in Little Orchard Street, which in 1862 sold nearly 3,000 quarts of soup to the poor at 1½d. or 1d. a pint. In 1866 a similar kitchen was opened in Carlton Street. At the north end of Alfred Street was the Christ Church Mission Room, now the Parish Hall.

A branch of the Church of England Temperance Society had been formed in the town and this gave the impetus for the opening of the British Workman, a café and temperance club, in 1876 in Meadow Street. In 1879

60   The National School at the bottom of Lower Church Road.

the Star Coffee House opened on the corner of Meadow Street and Alfred Street. It was originally a 'fourpenny dosshouse' offering cheap lodgings to vagrants, pedlars and poor workers. Later voluntary workers from Christ Church turned it into a cheap but respectable temperance hotel; a blazing fire was maintained winter and summer. Its thick 'doorstep' sandwiches were well known, and it sold bottles of hot tea to men on their way to work in the early morning.

A great proportion of the energies of Church and Chapel went into schooling for local children. At first this was the monopoly of the Church of England. The 1822 *Guide* mentions a school room for a hundred children, which had recently opened. In 1835 Henry Law, the Rector, was active in founding what became the Emmanuel Infants School, which was run on voluntary subscription until 1894. Ten years later the National School was opened at the bottom of Lower Church Road (now

part of the College site); pupils paid 2d. a week, or 1d. if more than one child from a family attended. An appeal for contributions was made to visitors because their presence during the summer months 'created a demand for juvenile labour to attend donkeys'; in the winter they relied on the charity of residents and these boys 'thrown adrift on the world should have the advantage of a sound religious education'.

Dissenters were becoming active in education during the 1840s. A Mechanics Institute, for adults, opened in 1846 under the presidency of the Rev. Mr. Hopkins, minister of the Independent Church. After a false start in 1851, the British School (under the auspices of the British and Foreign Schools Society) was built in Hopkins Street in 1855. John Palmer the builder donated the land, and most of the original committee were local tradesmen: Joseph James, another builder, James Harvey, bathing machine proprietor, Joseph Sturge, ironmonger, Henry Pond, brightsmith,

John Rossiter, watchmaker, Henry Langdon, licensed victualler. Funds remained a problem, and the fees of 6d. a week were high compared with the National School's. Nevertheless there were 137 children on the books by 1858, with 90 in average attendance.

The Church of England's influence remained predominant. In 1859 Miss Salter, sharing the perennial concern about the donkey boys, set up a night school in a room in Carlton Street, assisted by Mr. Mable, a cobbler, and this developed into the Albert Memorial School (1863) next to Emmanuel Church; the building was demolished to make way for the Town Hall extension. In the same year the Christ Church Elementary School opened.

Rivalry between the religious parties was intensified after Forster's Education Act of 1870, which pointed towards the principle of compulsory education for all children, to be secured if necessary by the establishment of local schools boards. Mr. A. Hutson has charted in detail the complex manoeuvres of the Church of England in Weston, which successfully delayed the establishment of a Board for 23 years. Fear of a rise in the rates played a part, together with desire for control of religious teaching. The Anglicans controlled three-quarters of Weston's school places, and moved swiftly to provide more following a notice from the Education Department which found the total insufficient: a new building next to the Christ Church School opened in 1874, the 'United Infants'. The cases for and against a School Board were eagerly canvassed in the local press.

The most remarkable element in the Anglican tactics was positive action to keep the British School open. The British School was in financial difficulties in the mid-'70s, but if it had closed the loss of school places in the town would have made it impossible to keep the spectre of a Board at bay. A relatively modest outlay averted this threat. Extensions were built to the National School in 1879, and to Christ Church, to keep pace with the growing population, but finally the financial strain of keeping up this race against numbers was too much. A School Board was finally established in 1893, and took control of some of the existing schools.

It took four years to build the first Board School, in Walliscote Road. Hans Price designed the splendid building, which has been described as one of the finest Board Schools in England. The second Board School was built in Locking Road (close to the unfinished St Saviour's) in 1900. In 1903 control of local education passed to Somerset County Council.

Hans Price also designed the School of Science and Art in Lower Church Road, the first proper higher education establishment, with large studio windows on the north side, although classes had been undertaken for some years previously. In 1900 the Museum and Public Library opened in The Boulevard; a museum collection had been kept in the Albert Memorial Hall for some time. The new building was partly paid for by public sub-scription and partly by a bequest of Mr. Frederick Wood of Chew Magna, who also donated his reference library, valued at £4,000, and promised to leave a legacy of £1,000 to the town if a suitable building were erected. The building was extended in 1932.

Side by side with the schools for local children there were numerous private schools for the children of the better off which flourished in the resort's healthy climate. Many were quite small, occupying villas built as private dwellings. Among the larger schools were Eastern House in Landemann Circus, and the College, purpose-built in Beach Road by Jonathon Elwell (subsequently converted into the *Grand Atlantic Hotel* after enlargements). F.A. Knight, whose books on the Mendip Country remain classics, was a teacher at Brynmelyn in Landemann Circus. Weston attracted private schools not only because of its climate, but because it was respectable and genteel. There were at least thirty private schools in Weston before the First World War and their disap-pearance only began after the Second.

61 *Above*. The Board Schools in Walliscote Road, built in 1897 'on the Prussian model'.

62 *Left*. The School of Science and Art. On the north side are large studio windows and the façade incorporates decorative ceramic tiles.

63 *Above right*. The Public Library in The Boulevard. The façade has statues by Henry Hems.

64 *Right*. The College, Beach Road, before it was enlarged as the *Grand Atlantic Hotel*; one of many private schools in Weston.

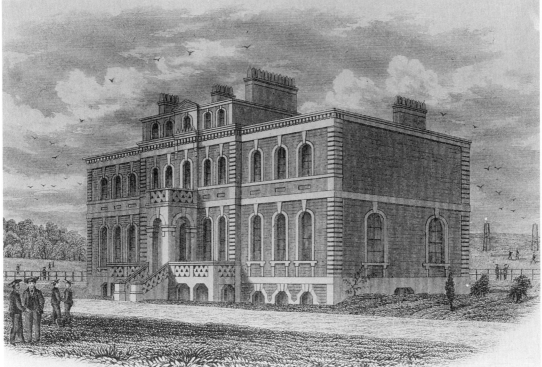

65 The Royal West of England Hospital seen from its grounds that stretched to the sand dunes.

Medical provision was limited to private doctors and a dispensary until the 1860s, when a subscription was opened for the building of a hospital. The move followed a serious accident to a building workman. Hans Price designed the original building on glebe land in Alfred Street. Other wards were added in the following decades, and in the 1920s a fresh campaign led to the new General Hospital, adjoining the original but facing The Boulevard.

Price had also designed part of the Royal West of England Hospital, known as the Sanatorium, as the south end of the Esplanade, which opened in 1868.

Hans Price gave to the town a collection of public buildings displaying individuality of style and civic dignity. With such commissions he was free from the constraints of domestic architecture and could give fuller expression to his interest in blending and experimenting with elements from different styles. Public buildings perhaps typify the Victorian period more than any other, but at a time when architecture always ran the risk of being debased through a preoccupation with gimmickry and detail, Price showed that ornament, however profuse, could still be used to create an overall effect and blend with earlier buildings. Most of Price's public buildings are now listed. To those already mentioned should be added others which are also 'public' in character, such as the Kew Masonic Lodge in The Boulevard (now the Constitutional Club), which has lost the wooden turret that was formerly such an idiosyncratic contribution to the skyline. On the opposite corner, close to the St John's Church Hall, is the building Price designed for the *Weston Mercury* in 1885. It is still used by the paper, which absorbed its rival, the *Weston Gazette*, in the 1950s.

The most obvious of Price's public buildings is the Town Hall. Weston's Commissioners had met at first in borrowed premises but chose the site for a town hall in the 1850s. Controversy soon erupted, however, because the land was on the northern fringe of Richard Parsley's old Whitecross Estate, which had been acquired by Joseph Whereat and Henry Davies. As Davies was the Clerk to the Commissioners it was felt that this was a move to enhance his new investment. Work began in 1858, but the dispute was not settled until the Rector, Archdeacon Law, bought the new building and made a free gift of it to the town in the following year. It is now incorporated into the larger complex, undertaken in 1897 to a design by Price, who remodelled the 'Big Ben' clock tower and added the entrance loggia and southern wing; a further addition of 1927 masks the original building beneath the tower. These elements achieve a confident unity and presence; this is how a public building ought to look, whatever the particular style. The Commissioners, who had previously taken on the functions of a Board of Health, had given way to an Urban District Council in 1894.

The town's public buildings mark half a century of expansion, confidence and achievement, at a time when the nation's optimism and wealth found unique expression in the seaside. As well as the buildings, the spaces between them tell the same story, for parks and gardens are parts of the fabric of the town, created to cater for residents and visitors who expected quality in their surroundings. The first wave of landscaped gardens was created in the

66 The offices of the *Weston Mercury* in Waterloo Street, designed by Hans Price in 1885 and still used by the local newspaper.

67 *Above left*. The Town Hall of 1858, and behind it Emmanuel Church in Oxford Street.

68 *Above*. The Town Hall, 1986. Hans Price extended and remodelled the building for the new Urban District Council in 1897, adapting the campanile as a clock tower. The northern block below the tower was added in 1927.

69 *Left*. Prince Consort Gardens being planted. Wattle fences were used to protect trees and shrubs from the sand and salt of the prevailing westerly winds. It required great labour to establish gardens in areas close to the sea.

residential suburbs: the Shrubbery, Eastfield Park, Park Place, Ellenborough Park. In the later years of consolidation that followed housing-led development, public parks appeared on the scene. Flagstaff Hill was turned into the Prince Consort Gardens soon after the opening of Birnbeck Pier in 1867, which brought new activity to this end of the hillside. In 1883 the town acquired the site of Clarence Park through the generosity of Rebecca Davies, widow of Henry. Following the opening of the new railway station, Old Station Square eventually became the Plantation, re-christened Alexandra Gardens (1909). The Recreation Grounds were opened on the other side of the new station in 1885. Ashcombe Park was laid out with grand avenues, the site having been safeguarded some years before.

In 1889 the Smyth Pigott family decided to leave The Grove, and it was at first proposed to sell the site for building; such was the public outcry that the grounds were acquired by the town for a yearly rent charge of £300 and Grove Park as we know it was created, with the bandstand and shelters that were soon provided. In the 1890s the public crowded into what had once been the squire's exclusive preserve, and the great era of open-air concerts began. By this time the grandest of all the open spaces in the resort had been laid out, the Beach Lawns, part of an ambitious seafront improvement scheme. Thus within a decade the town had acquired very significant additions to its green open spaces and further enhanced the quality of life and leisure both for visitors and residents.

Chapter Five

Seafront Schemes

WESTON BAY inspired numerous schemes of improvement and exploitation throughout the 19th century, some of which were actually implemented.

Landing boats was a problem at Weston because of the distance the tide recedes, and this was a difficulty at other seaside resorts which were not old ports. Piers were developed initially to solve this problem. Ryde Pier (1813–14), which extended 1,250 ft. into the sea, was a great success because of the new steamers, and others soon followed. At Weston, Knightstone became a kind of pier after its causeway was built up but even so the hours during which boats could land here were limited.

Steamers used both Anchor Head and the Axe Estuary as traffic increased during the 1840s. The first steamer to run an excursion from Weston was the *Sampson*, a tug, chartered by Captain Stone in 1843. Old paddle tugs were often more generously built than later ones, and were fitted with additional platforms and awnings when used for pleasure trips.

In September 1845 Captain Coles chartered the *Air* to take 140 passengers from Weston to Newport, and in the following year chartered her for the first Weston to Minehead excursion. Such trips were special occasions in the days before regular services became established, highlights of the local season, as this description of an excursion from Brown's *Weekly Advertiser* of 1847 illustrates:

The beach was lined with spectators. The vessel is the *Air*. She is a very fine boat, and admirably fitted up for passengers. She sailed about nine o'clock, having on board about 250 highly respectable visitors, and residents. The whole of the Swiss band was in attendance, and the fineness of the weather and the beautiful scenery of the Channel, and ever and anon the peals of music swelling on the breeze, must have rendered the excursion extremely delightful for those on board. The party returned to Weston about 9pm.

The success of the Channel steamers led to speculation about the wider commercial possibilities. While Brunel's Bristol and Exeter Railway was still under construction in 1841 the Bristol General Steam Navigation Company had begun building an iron steam vessel, the *Taff*, for 'the station between Uphill and Cardiff'. The following year the press carried advertisements for the project to 'unite the Taff and Exeter Railways'. 'The establishment of a general carrying trade throughout the Channel affords almost certain success to the undertaking', said the notice, adding that every possible encouragement short of a monopoly would be given to anyone who would establish a regular service. Nevertheless the scheme fell through, although it was the forerunner of several similar projects.

In 1845 the Weston-super-Mare Packet Station, Landing Pier, and Slip Company was formed with £40,000 capital raised through £50 shares. John Hugh Smyth Pigott was

70 James Dredge's proposed chain pier, 1845. This would have been a suspension bridge linking Birnbeck Island and the mainland. It would have been only the second chain pier in the country.

chairman, with 20 shares, and offered to give the necessary land and approach roads and whatever stone and wood were required. Other prominent Weston figures involved included Richard Parsley, William Cox, Francis Hutchinson Synge, and Joseph Whereat. The engineer was James Dredge of Bath, whose plans were approved by a public meeting held in the Temperance Hall. Sketches originally issued by the Company had shown a stone jetty south of Birnbeck Island, but Dredge proposed a chain pier or suspension bridge between the island and the mainland, with a span of 545 feet. Work had started on Brunel's great Suspension Bridge at Clifton in 1840, and Dredge himself had unsuccessfully entered designs for this project. There was only one chain pier in the country, at Brighton (1822-3). Suspension chains hung from cables between massive towers, and the deck hung from the chains, the ends of which were anchored at each end beyond the towers. In general chain piers did not catch on, but the fact that there was an island at Birnbeck, where the seaward end could be anchored, made this an attractive solution for Weston.

The Birnbeck chain pier was defeated by the sheer force of the currents. The first of the great stone pillars was washed away by the tide. Work was restarted, and in April 1847 Dredge undertook to finish the work in 12 months at a cost of £10,000, to be paid in instalments. August 1848 saw the company taking legal action to recover its money from the engineer. The work was far from finished and, having been again abandoned, was now useless. The company was awarded damages of £1,400. A local poet supplied the epitaph for the ill-fated project:

> Alas for the Pier! That wonderful Pier!
> 'Twas to bring Westonians some thousands
> a-year;
> Ships, schooners, and brigs all in multitudes
> here
> Were to come from Japan, and South
> Wales, and Cape Clear;
> And steamers by dozens were soon to
> appear.

Another ambitious scheme was launched in 1854. The Weston-super-Mare Pier, Steam Ferry, and Railway Company raised £20,000 in £10 shares, proposing to lay a railway line three-quarters of a mile long from the main line to a pier at Uphill, where the port would be equipped with warehouses, and hydraulic cranes. Francis Hutchinson Synge (who lived at Weston Lodge at the bottom of Lower Bristol Road) was again prominent in the venture. This was an era of unparalleled industrial expansion; it was the High Noon of Victorianism, and the growth rate exceeded any that had previously been known, or that has been known since. Development projects were in the air everywhere.

The next bout of optimism reverted to the north end of the bay. By this time Weston's Lord of the Manor was the irascible John Hugh Wadham Pigott Smyth Pigott, an enthusiastic patron of the Weston Regatta who suffered great humiliation because of the resort's inadequate landing facilities. During the regatta of 1856 the winds were such that, after the event, five of the gentlemen taking part were unable to land in order to attend the public dinner marking the occasion. Worse still, the winner of the cup was prevented from landing, and was thus unable to receive the company's congratulations. In 1859 Pigott and his associates produced another plan, for a solid masonry embankment curving southward from the mainland towards the southern tip of Birnbeck. 'It will turn the current which now flows so rapidly at every ebb and flood in its confined space, and render the actual basin a perfectly safe, and well sheltered harbour, sufficiently capacious to hold a fleet of from fifty to sixty sail.' A railway would run from just

above the new jetty to the main line at Puxton, and there would be a lighthouse on the island. Optimistic predictions were made about the effects of the altered currents on the sand and mud in the bay. The scheme would result in Weston and the neighbourhood 'becoming a great entrepôt of mineral, and other traffic'. Like its predecessors the project came to nothing.

Attention again veered to the south of the bay, but this time the speculators had learnt the lesson that they needed deep water. Uphill was abandoned in favour of the headland of Brean Down across the Axe Estuary. The Brean Down Harbour Company was incorporated in 1861 with capital of £350,000. The chairman was Sir John Eardley Wilmot of Swiss Villa. Again the idea hinged on prospects of commercial traffic between South Wales and the West of England: agricultural produce from the West Country would be exchanged for coal from South Wales. Experts testified before a House of Commons Select Committee to the immense scope for such trade. It was planned to build a breakwater at the end of Brean Down on the north side, and to connect the docks there with the main line by a railway running along the headland. The landing slip was to be 11,000 ft. long and 35 ft. broad, and there would be three divisions of docks giving a total wharfage of one and a half miles.

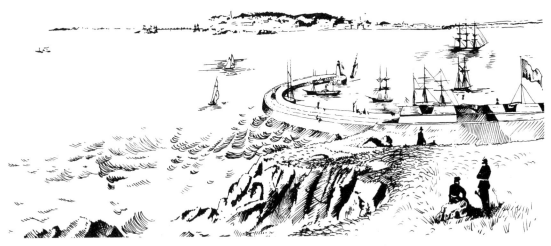

71   The proposed harbour at Brean Down, 1864.

72   Birnbeck Pier, built to Eugenius Birch's designs 1864-7. The site afforded deep water anchorage at all tides.

Work began at about the same time as construction of a nearby military installation, the Brean Down Fort, on the very tip of the Down. Palmerston's government had responded to scares about a possible French invasion and French innovations with iron-clad battleships by commissioning a string of new coastal defences, including four sites which between them would command the Bristol Channel approaches to Bristol and Cardiff: Lavernock in Wales, Steep Holm, Flat Holm, and Brean Down. The present 'military road' along the Down was built to serve the fort, which remained in use until it was partially destroyed by an explosion in 1900. Lady Eardley Wilmot had laid the foundation stone for the harbour on 5 November 1864, in front of a party of celebrities and the town band who had crossed

in a paddle steamer, the *Wye*. Unfortunately the stone was too light, and the next morning both the stone, and its marker buoy were found to have floated out to Steep Holm. Despite this inauspicious beginning work continued until a violent storm in December 1872 destroyed the jetty. The scheme was revived in 1887 but sufficient capital could not be raised. This was the most spectacular of the disasters that attended the many projects for Weston Bay.

'It would appear almost incredible that a watering place so matured in its pretensions, so conveniently situated, and so well frequented as Weston-super-Mare, should to this day be without a pier'. So began the prospectus, issued in 1864, of the company that was to succeed where others had failed and secure the building of Birnbeck Pier.

The Lord of the Manor was again a director of the new company, but this time his highly competent agent, Robert Landemann Jones, was the Chairman. Mr. Baker the solicitor was Secretary. The new management team was in charge. Two thousand shares were offered at £10 each. The components of the pier were prefabricated by Richard and John Laybourne at their Isca Foundry at Newport. It was probably a blessing in disguise that Weston had had to wait for its pier so long. In the event the town secured the services of the most famous pier builder of the age, Eugenius Birch, and obtained a structure which used the latest technology, capable of overcoming the difficulties posed by the strong currents. By this time Birch (1818-1884) was pre-eminent in the field. He had gained experience as a railway engineer in this country and in India, and indeed his career illustrates how the technology of Victorian industrialism could produce 'spin-offs' for the leisure market which developed during the century as its mirror image. Building Margate Jetty in 1853 Birch had pioneered the use of screw piles for driving the uprights into the seabed. He was to design 14 seaside piers altogether, including Blackpool North, Brighton West, Aberystwyth, and Eastbourne. It was his achievement to develop the promenade pier proper. Earlier piers had been largely bare, and devoid of interest above deck. At Brighton Birch took his inspiration from the Royal Pavilion (and perhaps from his memories of India), and created the ornate and vaguely Oriental architecture which is the hallmark of the classic pier, and of so many other seaside buildings. Brighton and Birnbeck were under construction simultaneously, and have important similarities, but, whereas Brighton Pier has received substantial later additions, Birnbeck is much as Birch designed it.

Piers exploited Britain's lead in civil engineering during the Victorian era. The solid masonry jetty was replaced by an open lattice-like structure, which was cheaper and offered little resistance to the tide; it also made moorings safer. The use of iron was the breakthrough. Timber in the sea is liable to attack by marine worm in a surprisingly short time. Cast iron became *the* material, strong in compression, and very resistant to corrosion if of good quality. The iron columns were cast circular, making them less resistant to currents than square ones. At Birnbeck the columns are in 15 clusters of four, mortised into the rock to a depth of three or four feet. The columns in each group are linked by tie rods twisted round each other in the centre of the tower, an unusual arrangement.

From an engineering point of view the system of struts and ties is considered to be especially interesting; this provides rigidity, harnessing the forces of tension and compression. For these joists wrought iron was the ideal material, lighter than cast iron, and having a different torsional strength. The deck is of wood, allowing for drainage. The main pier is 1,040 ft. long and over 20 ft. wide. The northern arm, the actual steamer jetty, continued to incorporate wooden piles to absorb the shock from boats docking.

The approaches were blasted through solid rock. At the laying of the foundation stone an awkward question of precedence arose between the notoriously aristocratically minded Lord of the Manor and the 'upstart' Commissioners. This was solved by having the ceremony performed by the squire's young son, Master Cecil Smyth Pigott, and he also officially opened the pier on 5 June 1867. The day was a general holiday. As well as the official dinner in the Town Hall, another was held at which six hundred sat down to eat in the Market Hall. Admission to the pier originally cost one penny, but the price was doubled at the end of the first season after 120,000 people had been admitted in three months.

Although there was great rejoicing at the pier's opening, it soon became obvious that the venture was not going to prove a rapid commercial success. The rail connection

73 & 74   Details of Birnbeck Pier's ironwork. Birch used the cast-iron components in a design that achieved great rigidity by calculating the forces of tension and compression.

envisaged in the early plans had not materialised. Birnbeck relied very heavily on the leisure market. Maintenance costs were high and profits low. The Pavilion and Reading Room were only completed in 1884, but the unique feature of Birnbeck Pier—its island—meant that these could be real buildings in stone. Also in 1884 the 'made ground' on the island was asphalted, and a tramway was built to carry luggage from the steamers. Three years later a switchback was in use, one of numerous 'fairground' amusements that crowded the island in the late Victorian and Edwardian heyday.

In 1893 Campbells chartered an old iron paddle steamer, the *Sea Breeze*, to establish themselves on the Weston-Cardiff run, and there was a period of spirited competition between Campbells and Edwards and Robinson of Cardiff. On one occasion two boats, the *Ravenwood* and the *Lorna Doone*, collided while racing for the jetty. It was common for rival boats to try to beat each other to landing points

around the coast in order to attract the bulk of the waiting passengers. Gradually Campbells, with their experience of operating on the Clyde, gained the upper hand. Their White Funnel Fleet—the 'swans'—dominated the Channel steamer trade in later years. A lifeboat station had opened on the north side of the pier in 1881, the boat being slung from davits until a boathouse was built in 1889. The second boat house was built on the south side, for easier launching, in 1902, and this still functions. It has the longest slipway of any lifeboat station in the country.

In 1892 a new low water steamer jetty opened to the south of the island, to cope with the increased volume of traffic. There were sometimes half a dozen vessels waiting to unload. It was estimated that an average August Bank Holiday might bring boats landing 15,000 people. In 1898 a new jetty was opened on the south west, 125 ft. long, and this was used until it was destroyed in the great gale of 1903.

75 Details from the Isca Foundry's ironwork in the canopy of Birnbeck Pier's Pavilion.

76 A steamer approaching the jetty at Birnbeck. This was a form of transport second only to the railway in importance during the resort's heyday.

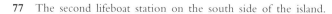

77 The second lifeboat station on the south side of the island.

78 Amusements on Birnbeck at the end of the 19th century. The clock tower was an important feature in the days of a busy steamer timetable.

Its replacement was in use from 1910 to 1916. The north jetty was also rebuilt after the gale, this time in steel, and was extended to 300 feet.

By the end of the century Birnbeck Pier was clearly prosperous. More and more people were able to take holidays, and travelling to the seaside was cheaper. Vast numbers of Welsh miners came to Birnbeck on steamer trips; many, on landing, got no farther, never entering the town at all but remaining on the island. The bar was one attraction, and others included tea and coffee rooms, a band, photographic studios, bazaars selling souvenirs, shooting galleries, swings, and (rare in those days) a telephone. The Pier Company had its own bye-laws to control behaviour. In 1894 there were 35 bye-laws, 18 of which carried penalties ranging from £2 to £5. Visitors were forbidden to 'halloo, shout or call out, or blow, strike or sound any gong, horn or other instrument, or

make any other noise beyond that of ordinary speaking'. On Boxing Day 1897, fire destroyed the main buildings including the concert hall, pavilion, and refreshment rooms. It is a sign of the company's healthy state at this time that, at 9 o'clock next morning, Hans Price's practice was instructed to draw up plans for rebuilding. The new buildings opened in July 1898. They incorporate columns from the Isca Foundry, and are impressive in their own right, worthy of the pier, and worthy of Price.

Birnbeck's eventual prosperity, after its faltering start, reflected the fortunes of the resort as a whole. The same determination to fight back against recession and to adjust to new markets produced the most impressive monument of all. The Seafront Improvement Scheme created the present appearance of the resort's waterfront. The earliest part of the scheme to be proposed was the levelling of the 'tots' or sand dunes and their replacement by gardens;

79 The first transatlantic telegraph cable is brought ashore at Weston in 1885. It ran to Waterville in Ireland, and from there to Newfoundland. From the cable office in Richmond Street two land lines ran to London and a third to Liverpool and Scotland.

an undertaking that something of this sort would be done had been given earlier in the century to the owners of the Whitecross Estate, where Ellenborough Crescent and other properties were being built. The dunes caused great problems because of drifting sand. However, the scheme as it actually took shape was first mooted by Edwin Knight, Chairman of the Local Board of Commissioners, at a private dinner. In December 1879 the Board appointed a committee to undertake the negotiations.

The resort was at a crossroads. There were many empty houses. The nationwide recession of the 1870s had left many unemployed, especially in the building trades which had enjoyed boom years at Weston during the resort's earlier period of rapid growth. Some of the upper classes were abandoning Weston in favour of more remote watering places such as Torquay, where the railways and the excursionists had not yet penetrated. Weston was attracting more and more people, but of a lower class; if they were to be accommodated, more space had to be opened up. Was the town to act positively to cater for the new market or was it to rest on its laurels? Mr. Knight offered the Seafront Improvement Scheme as a 'boon to the working classes', and one which could be carried through more cheaply during a recession than at any other time.

The Board had to secure government sanction for the borrowing of £28,000, and before this was obtained the whole idea had stirred up violent local controversy.

> During the whole course of these difficult negotiations there was great opposition to the whole scheme, and some extraordinary antagonistic plans were exhibited. Absurd rumours were freely circulated; persons who were in favour of the scheme being carried out were frequently met with derision; a Ratepayers' Protection Association was established, and every effort was made to effect the abandonment of the project. But an election of Commissioners taking place, all the candidates favourable to carrying out the work were returned ...

500 people attended an excited public meeting in the Town Hall on 27 April 1881. It was said that the scheme was not what was needed; that it was too expensive; that there had been too much secrecy; that the wall would be washed away; that there should be a choice of plans. Much of the criticism focused on the creation of 'artificial' flower gardens, with fountains, trees, shrubs, cascades, and kiosks. It was said that the plants would be blighted by sea winds in such an exposed situation, and that the cost of upkeep and constant replacement would be colossal; it would be better to create 'a greensward for cricket, and football exercises'. A resolution opposing the scheme was overwhelmingly carried.

The result of the Enquiry held in February 1882 was that a reduced loan was sanctioned subject to the plans for the gardens being dropped. On 15 March 1883 the Lord of the Manor, Cecil Smyth Pigott, laid the foundation stone in Glentworth Bay. Altogether the work was to require 175,000 tons of ballast, stone, and material; 85,000 cubic yards of earthwork infilling; 20,000 cubic yards of masonry; 9,000 yards of metalling; 49,000 yards of asphalting, and 4,000 yards of iron runner fencing. The engineer was Mr. T.J. Scoones of Bristol, who was already working in the area for the Great Western Railway. The contractor was Mr. Krauss of Bristol. The project was one of the biggest civil engineering undertakings of its kind in the region, and all the work had to be carried out between tides. It was considered a great feat that the whole of the foundations (on terrain varying from rock to clay and quicksand) were got in without the use of cofferdams. The work was always vulnerable, and there was one major setback, a bad gale on 17 October 1883, which destroyed about a quarter of a mile of the wall; debris was strewn down Regent Street and West Street. Yet the main scheme was completed in under three years.

There were three main elements: the replacement of the sand dunes by lawns; a

80 Early occupants of one of the seafront shelters.

81   A view of the bay, *c.*1890. The wide promenade and simple stone wall blend to enhance the dramatic vistas.

82   Glentworth Bay, *c.*1890.

carriage road; and, by the sea wall itself, an esplanade. The last two were carried out 'into the sea' over the beach by as much as 40 ft. in some places, and this explains the drop down to the sands from the promenade. The work stretched from the Royal West of England Hospital to Glentworth Bay, and was almost immediately extended northward to Birnbeck Pier; a length of some two and a half miles. It is well known that the tide rise here is the second highest in the world. To devise a scheme that could withstand the Atlantic gales, look stylish, and create space for thousands of visitors was a major achievement, especially in an age when work was still done by hand without the benefit of modern machinery.

The fact that all the elements were carried through as a complete scheme, on the grand scale, is what makes it so impressive a monument. The overall simplicity of design was emphasised by the substitution of lawns for intricate formal gardens. The scheme is bold and dramatic, taking its cue from the curve of the bay, which it civilises without cluttering unduly. The parapet wall is of stone, and since Weston is a stone town (one of the very few resorts to enjoy a good local supply), this relates the sea front to the town behind, enforcing its distinctive character. At the northern end the wall rises with the hill like part of a medieval castle, giving a comforting impression of strength.

One can understand why some ratepayers had found the economics of the proposals daunting. The cost (less than £30,000) would be millions today. At the time Weston's population was only just over 13,000. The town's rateable value was not much more than £60,000. The project was a huge gamble but it paid off. It had been proposed to put between 2d. and 5d. in the pound onto the rates for three or four years. In the event, the immediate rise in rateable value and the generally increased prosperity enabled the work to be completed without adding to the rates.

It was the leisure-oriented projects that were successful rather than those inspired by industrial trade and commerce. With its new railway loop and station, the delayed developments at Birnbeck at last completed, and the seafront scheme, the town had become what we still see today, and the stage was set for the late Victorian and Edwardian heyday of the resort.

83 At Anchor Head and Birnbeck the sea walls reach an impressive height. This end of the improvement scheme has its own distinctive character.

Chapter Six

Work and Play

BY THE 1880s the resort was catering for large crowds. The nature of the seaside experience which it offered changed as more people were able to come here to enjoy it. The resort had received occasional crowds of visitors since the first excursion trains began coming in the 1840s.

The Bank Holiday Act of 1871 effectively meant that any hopes of winning the war against the crowds were doomed. Numbers continued to rise. At Whitsun in 1876, 10,000 visitors arrived at Weston by rail or sea. By the end of the next decade there were estimates of 18,000 visitors on the Whitsun and August Bank Holidays. On such occasions the town's population temporarily doubled.

Universal bank holidays were a symbol of a more slowly working change. Perhaps more significant in the long run was the spread of holidays with pay, enjoyed by a growing number of lower grade office workers, shop assistants, and some factory workers.

The numbers of lodging houses in the town grew to cater for the new class of staying visitor, and many ordinary working people in the resort took in lodgers to supplement the family income. Brown records in 1855 that landladies were meeting trains at the station to solicit custom, and were hanging signs outside their houses. It should be remembered that a high proportion of the local working class lodged with other working-class families, as census returns reveal, so that even without summer visitors there were many terraced

houses such as those in Alfred Street or Hopkins Street accommodating a dozen or more people throughout the year. In 1865 the *Weston Gazette* reported complaints of overcrowding in the common lodging houses, due to the large number of workmen staying in the town because of projects such as the new railway station, the Brean Down Fort, and the Harbour Scheme.

Local landladies worked hard during the season. In order to make the maximum income they would often give up their own bedrooms and sleep in armchairs or sofas. Their children might have to relinquish their beds, and sleep under the kitchen table. It was the custom for lodgers to buy their own food and bring it back to the house for the landlady to cook, and washing and cleaning were also expected. The 1887 *Directory* lists 161 lodging houses, mostly on or near the sea front; the 1903 *Directory* lists 265, spread all over the town. These figures are only the tip of the iceberg, however; hundreds of other families took in guests, both in the older terraced working-class streets and in the newer streets of 'villas' built in the later years of the century. Allowing for the change to 'bed and breakfast', the same pattern held good until well after the Second World War.

The upper classes could still find superior lodging houses or even rent a house for the season, or they could indulge the Victorian middle-class habit for staying in an hotel and enjoying a complete service. The 1887 *Directory* lists the *Royal*, the *Imperial*, the *Victoria*, the

Railway, the *Plough*, the *Claremont*, the *Queen's*, and the *Royal Pier*. There were also three temperance hotels: *Ford's* and the *Shaftesbury* in Magdala Buildings, and *John Lake's* at 3 Anstice Terrace (Alexandra Parade). The number of temperance hotels had risen to nine by 1903, and to 17 by 1913.

In 1889 there were new 'commodious buildings adjacent to the County Club' in Knightstone Road where 'bath and dressing rooms are considered indispensable adjuncts to sleeping apartments'. The same year saw the celebratory dinner of the new *Grand Atlantic Hotel* in Beach Road, an enlargement of The College. Its 'Scottish Baronial' turrets made it a familiar feature of Weston's sea front, and with 200 rooms it became the resort's only real *Grand Hotel*, fronting the new Beach Lawns, and Esplanade.

The large crowds at peak times caused fears among the residents about disorderly behaviour, which were not always groundless. The first Police Station was the home of the sergeant, in Plough Court off the High Street, and the lock-up adjoined his cottage. In 1859 the *Weston Mercury* described the conditions:

> The so-called lock-up for Weston-super-Mare is a black hole about eight feet square with an open privy in one corner. Even the police, upon opening the door of the pestilential den of a morning, are often attacked with sickness from the dreadful effluvia, which belches forth upon them. What the wretched inmates of this horrible hole must suffer, who have been confined for some 12 or 18 hours, our readers can well imagine. The place is a disgrace to any civilised community—no man of feeling would permit his dog to lie therein.

A public outcry followed this report, and at the investigation which followed the Poor Law Medical Officer reported that there was only one cell, in which as many as five people had to spend the night. The sexes could not be segregated. The cell was open to the public sewer, and the only light and ventilation came from a small aperture 18 in. by six and from

BRISTOL & EXETER RAILWAY.

CHEAP EXCURSION
TO
WESTON.

On MONDAY, MAY 31st, 1869,
A CHEAP EXCURSION
WILL RUN AS UNDER.

FARES TO AND FRO,
on this occasion,
COV. CARS.

LEAVING	A.M.	
Exeter - - - -	8. 0	
Hele and Bradninch	8.23	
Collumpton - - -	8.35	**1s. 6d.**
Tiverton Junction -	8.44	
Tiverton - - - -	8. 0	
Wellington - - -	9. 7	

Arriving at Weston about 10.30 a.m. Returning from Weston at 6 p.m.

The Tickets are not transferable, and are not available by any other Train or for any other Station.

NO LUGGAGE ALLOWED.

By order,

84 Advertisement for an excursion trip to Weston, 1869.

85 The Albert Boarding House at the north end of Beach Road.

WESTON-SUPER-MARE.
Grand Atlantic Hotel,
FACING THE OCEAN.

This magnificent Hotel has recently been opened; it is furnished in a most luxurious manner, and replete with every modern appliance. Very moderate charges; *special* terms for Winter Residents.—For tariff apply to MANAGER.

WESTON-SUPER-MARE is three hours and a half by rail from London, half an hour from Bristol, and is the healthiest and most bracing watering-place in England.

SPECIAL ATTRACTIONS.

Pure Air: Direct Atlantic Breezes. Inexhaustible Supply of Water. Splendid Sea Front Promenade, two miles in length. Extensive Sands—a Paradise for Children. Promenade and Landing Pier, with Pavilion. Steamboats to Cardiff and other Ports in the Bristol Channel. Boating, Sailing, and Bathing. 300 Acres of well grown Woods to ramble through. Summer and Winter Garden. Lawn Tennis Courts at the Hotel. Recreation Ground, with Best Cycling Track in England. Good Centre for Excursions to the far-famed Cheddar Stalactite Caves and Cliffs; Wells, Llandaff, and Bristol Cathedrals; Glastonbury Abbey and Tor; Woodspring Priory; Mendip and Quantock Hills, and the Bone Caverns of Banwell.

THE RATE OF MORTALITY FOR THE SEPTEMBER, 1888, QUARTER WAS 9·6 PER 1,000.

CLIMATE.

"The Climate is equable, with a mean winter temperature above that of London; it is only 2° lower than that of Torquay, whilst the air is decidedly more bracing and less humid than the latter place, and therefore suits a different class of invalids. The cases that derive especial benefit from Weston air are those re ulting from impaired nutrition, such as early stages of tubercular disease, chronic rheumatism, &c. The equable climate and extremely dry nature of the subsoil are also especially favourable to all disorders of a catarrhal character."—*Lancet.*

86   Advertisement for the *Grand Atlantic Hotel.*

perforations in the door. One sergeant had died and the families of other officers on the premises were continually ill. The town's police force numbered three men.

The Commissioners offered the use of the basement in the newly built Town Hall. There were only two cells here, but they had to serve until Divisional Headquarters were finally moved from Axbridge to a new Police Station in Oxford Street in 1891. Even the new Station had only three cells, and the Weston force had only eight men, rising to 15 by 1898. Bank holidays brought chaos, with free fights in the streets. 'The presence of the police in the town on Monday was to a great extent a matter of form', said the *Weston Mercury* after one such incident.

In 1844 Westonians had petitioned the House of Lords to limit the number of beer houses in the town, and there is no doubt that

drunkenness was a problem which exacerbated crowd trouble at holiday times as numbers of trippers rose. Weston had nearly forty public houses at the end of the 1880s, as well as other beer houses or 'Tom and Jerry shops'. Cider was much more in evidence than it is today, and the lethal effects of the local scrumpy probably found many visitors unprepared.

The ready availability of drink in the days before modern licensing laws, and the inadequacy of the police force, make it surprising that there was not more serious trouble than there was in the resort. The seaside was the great escape for working people from the country's industrial heartlands; inevitably they brought urban habits with them. Part of the attraction of places like Weston was a relative classlessness and anarchy compared with the regimentation and caste system of the factory town, a rare break from the normal routine of long hours of repetitive work. Some exhilaration and indulgence were inevitable.

Local people worked long hours too, at some times of the year at least, and at other times they might not have the means to drink too much even if they had the disposition. The great local celebration when ordinary Westonians could let their hair down was the 'Wessun Revel' held on the first Thursday after 24 June. The Hotel Field, where the Italian Gardens are now, was the scene of this festivity for many years and saw donkey races, gingerbread and sweet stalls, travelling shows, and similar attractions. Rufus Palmer remembered that 'on these occasions, treacle pies, ginger beer, spice, nuts, and gilded gingerbread besides dolls, and fancy goods, to say nothing of Punch and Judy, appeared in all their glory. We youngsters looked forward to the Wessun Revel for months'.

Gradually, as Weston catered for more and more crowds, attractions became established on the beach. There were more stallholders and showmen every year, for whom the wide expanse of sand was a ready-made setting. A few alfresco shows had been staged there in

87-89 *Above*: *The Railway Hotel*. *Below left*: *The Globe*, St James's Street. *Below right*: *The White Lion*, St James's Street.

90   The beach as market and funfair, *c*.1907.

the 1840s, and after the Revel moved there some of its ingredients became semi-permanent fixtures during the summer. The beach became a noisier and busier place. By the end of the century it was thronged with pierrots, black and white minstrels, fortune tellers, Punch and Judy, photographers, refreshments stalls, the Salvation Army, temperance speakers, performing animals, and souvenir stalls.

Like other aspects of the new popular market, this caused some concern. The congestion resulting from unlimited numbers of stalls led the Commissioners, and subsequently the Urban District Council, to introduce a system of licensing, but this was only gradually enforced. Sunday trading was forbidden. The stalls were mostly wheeled, and were often covered with striped awnings. In the seasons leading up to the First World War 30 were licensed. The central 'pitch' was opposite the ends of Oxford Street and Richmond Street, the part of the beach for which visitors arriving at the Railway Station would make a beeline, and this area remained the busiest part of the sea front in later years.

The crowds brought a greater air of informality during the later years of the 19th century, and, if one could no longer hope to enjoy romantic solitude in Weston Bay, there was still plenty of room away from the busy central area for those who wanted a quieter time. The 'Little Sands' in Glentworth Bay remained rather more genteel than the main beach, and Anchor Head remained a favourite area for children to scramble about exploring the rock pools for crabs. The new promenade, linked to the carriage road through Weston Woods to Kewstoke, made it easier for visitors to venture farther from the heart of town, and in 1890 a bus service was introduced, with fares of 1d. and 2d. Weston's shoreline offered a range of seaside experiences, and despite the more urban tone of the main sands one could still simply spend time enjoying being by the sea. The presence of dogs and small children guarantees plenty of free entertainment as Jacques Tati's films remind us.

Bathing was as important as ever, although subject to more regulation. Bathing machines continued in use throughout the 19th century, but there were always people who preferred not to use them. Bye-laws of 1869 permitted men to bathe without machines south of a fixed point on the main beach. However, no one was to bathe within 200 yards of the opposite sex. Bathers were to use machines if within a quarter of a mile of a dwelling house, and the machines for men and women were to be segregated and kept 200 yards apart. Attempts to enforce these rules strictly must have involved difficult feats of calculation during busy periods. Some arrests were made but, like other efforts to regulate the changing situation, these were only partly effective. One of those who disliked the regime of bathing machines was the Rev. Francis Kilvert, who stayed at Prince's Buildings in 1872. On 4 September he wrote in his diary: 'Bathing in the morning before breakfast from a machine. Many people were openly stripping on the sands a little further on and running down into the sea, and I would have done the same but I had brought no towels of my own.' The next day he joined the rebels: 'I was out early before breakfast this morning bathing from the sands. There was a delicious feeling of freedom in stripping in the open air and running down naked to the sea, where the waves were curling white with foam and the red morning sunshine glowing upon the naked limbs of the bathers.' When the machines were destroyed or damaged in the gale of 1903 they were not replaced, and had clearly already become old fashioned.

Donkeys were a perennial part of the sea-front scene. In village days they had been used as beasts of burden, being cheaper than horses, and among the early visitors their use was by no means restricted to children. It was common for ladies and the less dashing gentlemen to hire donkeys for quite extensive forays around the neighbouring countryside. Donkey carriages were popular with the elderly or infirm, as well as with children.

The donkeys appealed to the new crowds, who might not be very expert horsemen, as

the chance for 'a bit of fun'. The growing army of donkey boys was a continual source of worry, as we have seen, and they had only seasonal employment. At the turn of the century there were up to 100 donkeys on the beach and their stands were all along the sea front. Today bye-laws give the poor patient animals some protection by decreeing a six-day week, limiting rides to children, and limiting the distance of each ride to 100 yards, and back.

Live music was another essential ingredient. In 1857 there had been a demand for a promenade band to enable Weston to compete with Weymouth, and within a few years German and Italian Brass Bands were playing at numerous venues in the resort. Ellenborough Park often had band concerts. Concert parties were also very popular and could be found in Grove Park, Birnbeck Island, Madeira Cove, Clarence Park, and the Assembly Rooms. In the early years of the 20th century the outstanding figure was Harry Mogg, a former postman and self-

TERRIFIC GALE.

IRREPARABLE DAMAGE AT WESTON-SUPER-MARE.

SEA FRONT AND PIERS PARTIALLY WRECKED.

BOATS FLOATING ABOUT IN THE ROADWAYS.

ELECTRIC TRAM SERVICE STOPPED.

THOUSANDS OF POUNDS WORTH OF DAMAGE

BATHING MACHINES DEMOLISHED.

CELLARS AND BASEMENTS FLOODED.

TREMENDOUS SEAS AND MUCH WRECKAGE.

DISAPPEARANCE OF A WESTONIAN.

WHOLESALE DESTRUCTION.

A NEVER-TO-BE-FORGOTTEN SPECTACLE.

91 Report on the great gale of 1903.

92 & 93 Damaged bathing machines after the 1903 gale.

94 A local fishing boat or 'flatner' prepares to board passengers at Anchor Head for a trip round the bay, 1896.

taught musician who became proprietor of the Castle Coffee House, a well-known working men's meeting place in Castle Street, off Oxford Street. Mogg's Military Band had a long and glorious history, and won the 1912-13 National Challenge Shield at the Crystal Palace.

A great many people earned their livings from all these attractions and entertainments; but this crowded, jolly and lively scene lives on only in old photographs or anecdotes. The stalls and booths and makeshift stages were ephemeral, swept away over the years as they were always liable to be swept away by the high tides. In the crowded resort of the late Victorian and Edwardian years such attractions sprang up in a moment, whenever an enterprising trader or showman saw his chance. It was the people rather than the accommodation that mattered and, if this was all part of the change to an urban market, at least it brought out the best features of town life in an age when conditions in towns and cities were all too often grim and depressing. Here was colour, variety, life, which added to the resort's character and gave a counterpoint to the decorous stillness of the respectable suburbs.

95   An early charabanc outing.

96   Mogg's   Band   on
Knightstone, 1912.

97   A Weston Cycling Club rally, 1888.

Open-air sports had become more popular in the second half of the century, and flourished at the seaside. Tennis became popular, and many of the larger villas had private courts. In August 1888 the Lawn Tennis Championships, believed to be the first in Weston, were held on the courts of the new *Grand Atlantic Hotel*. The Beach Lawns had represented a victory for those wanting more space for cricket and other games. Bowls also had a following, and greens were provided in Clarence and Ashcombe Parks. The Weston-super-Mare Golf Club in Uphill Road North opened in 1892. Late Victorian Weston offered an impressive range of sporting opportunities to visitors and residents alike.

Entertainments began to be housed in more permanent accommodation. In 1882 the Summer and Winter Gardens opened on the north side of The Boulevard. They had a large promenading area under glass, reached through a very conspicuous entrance lodge reminiscent of a triumphal arch and designed by Hans Price. Beside the glassed area was the Victoria Hall and Opera House, capable of holding 800 people. This seems a determined effort to keep up the tone, but by the early years of the new century this private venture had been converted to a roller skating rink, with a cycling track, bowling green and tennis courts. The green was eventually bought by a bowling club which still uses it, and another part of the site was sold for a Masonic Hall. The Summer and Winter Gardens became a Palace of Varieties, then a theatre run by Carlton Fredricks, and finally the Tivoli Cinema, after substantial rebuilding. It was bombed in 1942 and remained derelict for 40 years until redeveloped as flats in 1983-4.

The early years of the new century saw Knightsone Island turned into a major new attraction. Beside the original Georgian Bath House handsome new public baths were built. They used sea water, taken in at high tide into a huge settling tank which is 'inside' the island. (Part of the island is 'made ground', won by levelling the surface and taking in additional space with the retaining wall.) The tank extends under the Pavilion or Theatre, which opened on the same day as the Baths, 13 May 1902. Both developments were undertaken by the local authority, which had acquired the island. J.S. Stewart was the architect of the Pavilion, and Krauss the engineer, who gave it 'practically indestructible foundations'. The Pavilion had refreshment rooms, a reading room, and billiard room 'to be popular with all classes'. It was planned originally for promenade band concerts, and

at first good bands were engaged: the Grenadiers, the Coldstream Guards, the Horse Guards, and the White and Blue Viennese Bands. There were also plays, and light opera. However the stage was too shallow for large productions. The building had electric light (a new convenience in the resort) and hot water heating. The island and causeway almost formed a second pier.

Almost immediately a second real pier did open, the Grand Pier opposite Regent Street, and this posed stiff competition both for Knightstone and Birnbeck. An Act of Parliament for a second pier had been obtained in 1893. Eventually £200,000 was subscribed for the venture and Messrs. Maych and Haley began erecting the iron columns in 1903. The superstructure was steel open work girders with traceried braces. In June 1904 the first 360 yards and the Pavilion were opened, and two years later a further 500 yards had been added. The Grand Pier was intended to be able to receive steamers: hence the tremendous length in the centre of the bay. In fact only three boats ever called. There was silting in the approach channels, and the currents were difficult. Steamer captains refused to land here. In 1914 the original company was compulsorily wound up, and two years later the extension was dismantled except for a length of 40 yards beyond the Pavilion.

98 The public baths at Knightstone.

99 A sketch of the proposed Grand Pier showing its intended length.

100 The original entrance to the Grand Pier.

The Grand Pier was virtually the last great pleasure pier built in this country. It eventually flourished as an entertainment centre. It was sited in the thick of the crowds, and boasted two refreshment rooms, shops, and a permanent bandstand as well as its Pavilion. Entrance was 2d. and the attractions in the early years included opera, music hall, musical comedy, Shakespearean drama, ballet, as well as more 'popular' attractions such as boxing or roller-skating. Mogg's Band was booked permanently for the bandstand, and Herr Kandt's Austrian Band for the Pavilion. The Grand Pier relieved the pressure on the busiest section of the sea front by providing an extension of it, and it underlined the fact that the resort's appeal now rested to an important extent on its wide and varied repertoire of live entertainment.

Chapter Seven

Between the Wars

THINGS WERE NEVER quite the same after the First World War. There was a new ethos, at the seaside as elsewhere; buildings, clothes, leisure habits all changed, and Weston adapted to the Age of the Common Man. There was still a sense of style, but it no longer derived from the traditional sources.

New buildings used different materials and techniques. The most obvious change was that local stone was hardly ever used; brick became the standard material, although pottery roof tiles were still in evidence. Houses built after 1918 no longer displayed a local character. Although Weston's population actually fell in the 1920s (the only decade in the town's history when it has done so) there was much new building during the inter-war years. Many of the new semi-detached houses were pebble-dashed or rendered over brick. There was ribbon development along Locking Road, and considerable expansion to the south and east of the old town. Houses were built more to the scale of the ordinary modern family, and individual examples are often attractive, with interesting decorative features such as stained glass; but, taken in the mass, they are less remarkable than the resort's earlier housing.

At Milton Green the local authority built the first public housing anywhere in the country, following Addison's Act of 1919.

101   Early council housing at Milton Green, showing the new approach to road layout.

Scattered about the town are a small number of private houses that adopt the 1930s fashion for a Mediterranean look: white painted render, interesting metal-framed windows, and in some cases flat roofs.

The Town Quarry was busier than ever, but mainly supplying material for the roads. As well as producing tons of rubble it met an increased demand for tarmac, as more and more roads were upgraded for motor vehicles. The period also saw the development of Henry Butt's quarry at Milton, and indeed the emergence of Butt himself as a dominating figure on the local stage. He was the quintessential 'local boy made good', who had come to Weston as a teenager from Langport, working for a local coal company. Within a few years he had hired a horse and cart and laid the foundations of his own prosperous carrier's business, dealing in coal, building materials, and general goods. He branched out to buy the Milton Quarry, and installed giant modern kilns which produced lime for cement and white-wash. Butt also became a builder in his own right, specialising in the conversion of larger Victorian villas into 'mansions' of flats, adding wings to the original buildings.

102   Private housing of the 1930s in Station Road.

103   Henry Butt, a dominant figure in Weston between the wars.

104   Lime kilns at Butt's Quarry in Milton.

Henry Butt lived at 1 Eastfield Park, and became a Justice of the Peace, a County Councillor, and a millionaire who gave away vast sums to charity. He entered into local mythology: the successful rough diamond who retained the common touch and never acquired the polish or style of the older élite. He would always carry cheap cigarettes which he gave out to his workmen, and pockets full of imitation jewellery which he gave them for their wives. By some sections of the local establishment he was cordially detested, but

there was no arguing with his drive or his money. Perhaps he brought home to the 'good' families how times were changing.

Butt was the driving force behind the local fund raising that made possible the building of the new General Hospital in the Boulevard. He personally spent many hours tramping round the town collecting donations or promises of money, ominously producing his famous black book in which to record a victim's response to his special combination of persuasion and blackmail. The hospital was practically the last major building in the town centre to use stone. It was opened by the Duke and Duchess of York (later King George VI and Queen Elizabeth) in 1927, and greatly extended the original Alfred Street buildings with which it connected. The new hospital had balconies opening off the wards, where convalescent patients could enjoy the sun and air. According to local legend Butt lost the chance of a knighthood at the opening when he lit a cigarette and blew smoke in the Duchess's face.

Butt had engaged in a long-drawn-out lawsuit with the Council concerning the damage caused by his heavy vehicles to the town's roads. His vehicles followed a triangular route between Milton Quarry, the Goods Station, and Knightstone Harbour where they collected coal. Butt fought the case all the way to the House of Lords, but lost. His reaction in defeat was wholly typical: as though to show no hard feelings he offered to meet the cost of acquiring the Hotel Field between High Street and the sea front for the purpose of laying out new Winter Gardens, a project which had been long debated in the town. The work began in 1924 and cost £16,000. The Pavilion was built in 1927 at a cost of £35,000; the low profile of the domed building was the result of negotiations over covenants protecting the sea views of properties on the opposite side of the High Street.

105   Winter Gardens Pavilion.

106 Winter Gardens Pavilion.

107 Building the Marine Lake Causeway at Glentworth Bay, 1929.

The Winter Gardens and Pavilion were one of a number of bold steps taken by the Council during the inter-war years to fight back against the effects of nationwide reces- sion. The new Pavilion became very popular as a venue for dancing and light orchestral concerts. The H.C. Burgess Orchestra was formed in 1920 for the summer season, and became permanent, playing regularly in the Winter Gardens Pavilion until 1938.

In 1929 the Council completed another scheme, the creation of the Marine Lake at Glentworth Bay through the building of a causeway from Knightstone. Together with the older causeway to the island it trapped the tide. This, too, was in tune with the popular mood. There was a new relaxed informality about dress and behaviour. Sunbathing and beach parties had become fashionable, following the new life style of the smart set in the South of France. The Marine Lake was equipped with a diving stage, rafts, rubber air boats, water chutes, childrens' paddle boats, as well as hundreds of

108 Bathers at the Marine Lake on the concrete walkway which was added, with a colonnaded extension to the promenade above, in 1937.

bathing tents and dressing enclosures. It was dedicated to fun. The whole project had been undertaken as a job creation scheme to help relieve unemployment in South Wales. Admission to the Lake was supposed to be controlled and one paid to go in and use the facilities. The Rozel Bandstand was added in 1937, a further extension of the colonnaded walkway around the edge of the Lake by the promenade. Following gale damage in 1981 the whole of this extension was demolished and the Victorian sea wall restored.

109 The new pavilion at the Grand Pier, built after the fire of 1930.

The Knightstone Pavilion during the 1920s offered cinema shows, plays, light opera and other shows. It attracted many repertory and touring companies. Rex Harrison, Paul Robeson, and Dame Clara Butt were among those who played here. The Grand Pier added amusements to its attractions in 1926, but its days as a venue for live entertainment were ended by a devastating fire in 1930. The Pier was subsequently bought by Leonard Guy, who had held the sideshows concession earlier and had been manager of the entertainments at Birnbeck. In 1932 rebuilding started above deck, but this time it was a funfair, not a theatre, that emerged. It was the largest funfair on any pier.

Weston had four cinemas by the end of the 1930s. The Winter and Summer Gardens in The Boulevard had been substantially re-built as the Tivoli in 1928, and there were also the Gaumont in Oxford Street and the Central in Regent Street. Most distinguished of all was the Odeon, built on the site of the old Electric Cinema in 1935. The architect was Cecil Howitt, who won an award for the design. The building is uncompromisingly of its period, with clean lines and simple shapes: a total rejection of the Victorian notion of what a public building should look like. The external cladding tiles also proclaim modernity. Yet the building was carefully designed for its corner site facing the open space of The Plantation, and its low tower, with flat projecting top raised on short round pillars, is a strong feature. Inside, the auditorium (now subdivided) was dominated by the illuminated console of the Compton Organ, which was often used for recitals and broadcasts.

Adjoining the Odeon is The Centre (rather hopefully named) facing Oxford Street, a curving row of shops which covered ground that had been open between the 1860s railway station and Town Hall. Unfortunately many of the details that were crucial to its design have been changed. Across the corner down Walliscote Road is the Police Station and Magistrates Court, a Classical Revival building of 1934. There are some interesting shops at the south end of the main part of the High Street, on the west side, which add to the variety of the street; Burtons, on the corner with Regent Street, is especially good. At the south end of the town and facing the timbered grounds of Uphill Castle was the Grammar School of 1935, with its central clock tower and quadrangles.

The Open Air Pool was built by the Council in 1937 and was the biggest in Europe. It had an Olympic standard 10m. diving stage in reinforced concrete, which dominated the

110 & 111   Cecil Howitt's Odeon (*above*) and Burtons in High Street (*below*) both are variations on themes used throughout the country by new national companies.

112 The clock tower of the former Grammar School in Broadoak Road.

113 The Open Air Pool's diving platforms were among the most striking examples of the modern style at Weston.

enclosed space. Under the diving stage the pool was nearly five metres deep. The pool held 850,000 gallons of purified sea water—and 1,500 bathers. There was also space for hundreds of sunbathers and spectators. In the early 1980s the diving stage was demolished and the Pool was redesigned as the Tropicana Leisure Centre.

The crowds were bigger than ever during these years, and grew throughout the period. At the beginning of the 1920s August Bank Holiday crowds might number 50,000, but by the end of the next decade they were nudging 80,000. There were more lodging houses than ever, stretching back down Locking Road. Charabancs and coaches brought more and more passengers, and were available for trips from the resort. In 1928 the mansion of Belvedere in Beach Road was demolished to make way for a Bus Station. Trams ran along the sea front and back to their Depot in Locking Road. They had appeared in 1902, the year after electricity came to the resort. The trams disappeared in 1937, unable to compete with the buses.

The private motor car was still relatively scarce, but it was growing in numbers, and many of the ancient lanes between the villages around Weston were straightened and widened to cater for increased motor traffic. The old route over the hill from Uphill to Bleadon was superseded by a cutting through the hill and a new section of road by-passed the village. The village of Locking was by-passed. Yet the railway still brought the majority of visitors. Excursion trains left Bristol every few minutes at peak periods, and hundreds flooded into Locking Road from the excursion platforms that stretched back from the Goods Station.

There was a special enjoyment to be derived from travelling on the Weston, Clevedon and Portishead Light Railway, which ran between 1897 and 1941. The 'Blackberry Line', as it was called, was the subject of much merriment. The Weston Station was at the junction of Milton Road and Ashcombe Road

and the line ran out to Milton and Worle, with two level crossings over the main Bristol Road, before heading off across the Northmarsh to Clevedon. The line was extremely useful for local people, and carried freight as well as passengers; it carried coal and collected the milk churns from isolated farms along the route, stopping at tiny stations such as Ham Lane and Wick Wharf. Like other light railways it was killed by cars and buses.

The development of bigger seafront attractions consolidated the popular image of the resort. The original importance of the town's setting, and the pleasures to be obtained from easy access to attractive countryside, began to fade from the picture. Nevertheless until well after the Second World War Weston was a place where the visitor might still be aware of the rural hinterland. One could walk out to open countryside within ten or fifteen minutes from anywhere in the town. The popular writer S.P.B. Mais began his chapter on Weston in *Walking in Somerset* (1935):

> Weston-super-Mare is at once one of the most amusing and most picturesque of popular seaside resorts. It is in consequence roundly abused by those who have never visited it. It is easily accessible by air, sea and land, and makes a very good centre for excursions to all parts of Somerset. It is, for instance, the obvious starting point for the Mendip Hills.

And in an era when the rights of popular access to the countryside were at last established, after battles in the 19th century and campaigns by the Ramblers Association, there were many enthusiastic hikers and ramblers who emulated Mais and explored the country around Weston. The walk to Kewstoke and Sand Bay was popular, perhaps including the Tea Garden at the top of Monks' Steps. One might venture beyond Uphill, use the ferry at the mouth of the Axe to cross to Brean. Or one could head inland to explore the still undeveloped villages of Hutton, Locking and Worle. Despite new farming methods and road transport, the countryside around the resort was far less

EVERY THURSDAY AND SATURDAY AFTERNOONS HALF DAY EXCURSION TICKETS WILL BE ISSUED FROM WESTON-SUPER-MARE TO CLEVEDON. FARE 9½d. RETURN.

CHEAP TICKETS issued DAILY by nearly all Trains.
WESTON-SUPER-MARE to CLEVEDON (and vice versa) 1/1 Return.

DOWN TRAINS.		WEEK DAYS.					SUNDAYS.
		a.m.	a.m.	p.m.	p.m.	p.m.	a.m.
Portishead	dep		10 15	1 35		4 45	
Portishead South	,,		10 18	1 38		4 48	
Clapton Road	,,		b	b		b	
Cadbury Road	,,		10 25	1 42		4 52	
Walton-in-Gordano	,,		10 29	1 46		4 56	
Walton Park	,,		b	b		b	
Clevedon (All Saints')	,,		10 33	1 50		5 0	
Clevedon East	,,		10 34	1 55		5 5	
Clevedon	,,	7 50	11 0	2 15	3 55	5 20	8 35
Colehouse Lane	,,	b	b	b	b	b	b
Kingston Road	,,	7 56	11 6	2 21	4 1	5 26	8 41
Broadstone	,,	b	b	b	b	b	b
Ham Lane	,,	7 59	11 9	2 24	4 5	5 29	b
Wick St. Lawrence	,,	8 5	11 13	2 28	4 8	5 33	8 49
Ebdon Lane	,,	b	b	b	b	b	b
Worle Town	,,	8 13	11 21	2 36	4 16	5 41	8 56
Bristol Road	,,	8 16	11 24	2 39	4 19	5 44	8 59
Milton Road	,,	b	b	b	b	b	b
Weston-super-Mare	arr	8 35	11 30	2 45	4 25	5 55	9 5

Sundays, Christmas Day & Good Friday

UP TRAINS.		WEEK DAYS.					SUNDAYS.
		a.m.	a.m.	p.m.	p.m.	p.m.	a.m.
Weston-super-Mare	dep	8 55	11 45	3 0	4 30	6 0	9 15
Milton Road	,,	b	b	b	b	b	b
Bristol Road	,,	9 1	11 51	3 6	4 33	6 6	9 21
Worle Town	,,	9 4	11 54	3 9	4 36	6 10	9 24
Ebdon Lane	,,	b	b	b	b	b	b
Wick St. Lawrence	,,	9 12	12 2	3 17	4 44	6 18	9 31
Ham Lane	,,	9 16	12 6	3 21	4 48	6 22	b
Broadstone	,,	b	b	b	b	b	b
Kingston Road	,,	9 19	12 9	3 25	4 51	6 25	9 38
Colehouse Lane	,,	b	b	b	b	b	b
Clevedon	,,	9 30	12 15	3 30	5 0	6 30	9 45
Clevedon East	,,	9 33	12 18	3 32	Stops	Stops	Stops
Clevedon (All Saints')	,,	9 34	12 19	3 33			
Walton Park	,,	b	b	b			
Walton-in-Gordano	,,	9 38	12 23	3 37			
Cadbury Road	,,	9 42	12 27	3 41			
Clapton Road	,,	b	b	b			
Portishead South	,,	9 46	12 31	3 45			
Portishead	arr	9 55	12 45	4 0			

Sundays, Christmas Day & Good Friday

b—Stops by Signal to pick up or set down passengers as required.

The Company reserve the right to withdraw any of the above trains without previous notice.

All Daily Cheap Tickets issued to and from Weston-super-Mare are available at Milton Road Station.

Cheap Tickets issued daily, Portishead to Weston-super-Mare, 1/10 Return.

(The Fares shewn are subject to increase or cancellation without previous notice)

Arrangements can be made for Special Large Parties at Reduced Fares.

Workmen's Tickets at Reduced Fares are issued daily to bona-fide Workmen, available to return by any train after 2 p.m. each day, and are available on day of issue only.

114   A timetable for the Weston, Clevedon and Portishead Railway, 1939.

touched by modernity than the town itself, and the old rural way of life subsisted practically on Weston's doorstep.

Nevertheless the value of the town's setting was ceasing to be appreciated by all its citizens, as became evident when Weston Woods came under threat. The Smyth Pigott Estate had been steadily selling off land since the turn of the century. It had retained the woods throughout this period, although they had been open for public enjoyment since the middle of the 19th century. In 1936 nearly 400 acres of the woods were offered to the local authority for £10,000 but the deal was turned down. Soon afterwards the land was sold to a syndicate for £19,500. A broad road along the top was opened from the eastern end to the Water Tower, and it was planned to

115   A tram on the sea front passing the end of Regent Street.

20,000
Passengers have flown at
Weston Airport
since June, 1936
and liked it !
—so will you.
JOYRIDES 5/-
WESTON — CARDIFF in 10 minutes
SERVICES EVERY HOUR—EVERY DAY.   6/6 Single, 9/6 Return.

★

Phone :
**WESTERN
AIRWAYS**
WESTON
2002

★

These are some of the sturdy De Havilland Dragons used by Western Airways on the Weston–Cardiff service—the machines you see continually overhead. You can smoke in them. Armchair comfort—hot and cold ventilation. Absolutely reliable and safe.

— VISIT THE AIRPORT THIS EASTER —
- *It is entirely open to the non-flying public* •

Come and see all the activity of an airport—the people and planes arriving and departing—people taking joyrides, and asking for thrills—and then perhaps you would like a joyride yourself—it only costs **5/-.**

TAKE LUNCH or TEA in the AIRPORT RESTAURANT or VERANDAH CAFE—
and watch the flying at the same time.

116   Advertisement for flights from Weston Airfield.

build houses along the top of the hill. Eventually the Council was shamed into action and managed to acquire fewer than 300 acres for £22,000, together with a section of the Jackson-Barstow Estate at Ashcombe. Most of the woods were saved, but it was impossible to stop building at the eastern end.

1936 also saw the opening of the Weston Airfield to the east of the town on Locking Moor, a development that put it briefly on the world map in terms of aviation. Colonel S.F. Cody had brought the first aeroplane to Weston in 1911, landing on the beach in front of the *Grand Atlantic*, and in the same year Mr. B.C. Hucks made the first of a number of flights across the Bristol Channel. Small planes frequently in the following years used the sands or nearby fields for landing and take-off. In the 1930s the Council gave approval for the building of a municipal airport, which was soon leased to Western Airways, and a brief period of cross-Channel flights began. These were immediately popular, and the service was taken over by the Straight Corporation in 1938. Whitney Straight was a pioneer of domestic air services, and under his direction the operation was expanded. New routes were added, even including occasional flights to Paris. On 2 October 1938 the first internal night service began, with floodlights on the Airfield. The service to Cardiff was by now half-hourly, which was claimed to be the most frequent anywhere in the world. Weston Airfield was the second busiest in the country. However in 1939, with war looming, the Air Ministry established a reserve centre at Weston, and the following year the Weston-Cardiff service was closed despite local objections. The fleets of aircraft, including De Havilland and Dragon biplanes, were requisitioned, and Weston's brief career as a major civil aviation centre was ended.

The Urban District Council, which had replaced the Commissioners, was itself replaced by a Borough Council in 1937. The Charter was presented in front of a large crowd at the Grove Park bandstand, and the first Mayor of Weston-super-Mare was, almost inevitably, Henry Butt. The proud new Borough took as its motto 'Ever Forward', and it must certainly have seemed as if the momentum of improvement and expansion was assured and unstoppable. The crowds would go on getting bigger than ever, the sun would shine in a cloudless sky, and the money would roll in. Yet at the very moment of achieving its coveted Borough status Weston was set to encounter problems. As the controversy over the Woods had presaged, the high point of civic pride and complacency contained the seeds of future difficulties. These were not to become apparent for some years, even after the war that was soon to come, but in many respects *this* was Weston's finest hour.

Chapter Eight

Modern Times

THE SECOND WORLD WAR saw a rapid build-up in the town of plant connected with wartime aviation needs. RAF Locking had begun as a hutted camp in 1938 and trained personnel in many skills. There were several 'shadow factories' near the Airfield. The Western Airways site became a factory producing aircraft and employing 300 local people; the twin engine canvas-covered Avro Anson 'bone-shakers', used by the RAF for pilot training, were built here. Bristol Aircraft Ltd. produced Bristol Beaufighters at their Oldmixon factory, and during the war 3,400 aircraft were built. The airfield itself was never 'operational', although it was a reserve site, and drainage improvements were carried out to the Uphill Great Rhyne to protect the area.

Important research was undertaken along the Weston coast. Birnbeck Pier became 'H.M.S. Birnbeck' and new weapons were tested here, as well as at Brean Down Fort and St Thomas's Head at Middle Hope. These included the 'bouncing bomb' devised by Barnes Wallis and used by the dambusters, which was to prove critical in defeating the threat posed by the German U-boats. Antiaircraft batteries, part of a ring protecting Bristol and the Channel approaches, were located near

117 Bristol Beaufighter production during the Second World War.

118 *Left*. The interior of St Paul's Church after the air raid of 1940.

119 *Above*. Bomb damage to a Weston villa.

Weston. One can still see the remains of some of these on Brean Down. Weston Woods were also used, and were out of bounds to local people for some time. In addition there were measures to prevent a beach landing by the enemy, with mines and barbed wire barricades. Weston's own 'Dad's Army', the Home Guard, occupied the same hilltop sites which had been look-out spots and beacon sites centuries before. The old windmill tower at Uphill was one observation post.

Weston may have gained a reputation in Germany as a munitions town, and some have attributed bombing on the town to this fact. The first bombs fell on Weston in 1940, but the first major air raid came on 4 January 1941, when 34 people were killed and 85 injured. Rector's Way, Stonebridge Road, Grove House, St Paul's Church and Whitecross Hall were among the sites hit, together with other shops and houses. Even more damage was caused the following year, on 28 and 29 June, when 10,000 incendiaries and more than 60 high explosive bombs fell on the town. More than 100 people were killed and 400 were

injured. The Tivoli Cinema, the Lance and Lance store on the High Street-Waterloo Street corner, the Boulevard Congregational Church, the Wadham Street Baptist Church, the Assembly Rooms and Marks and Spencer in the High Street were all hit, together with 3,500 houses damaged or destroyed. These raids were blamed by some on an article in the *News Chronicle* shortly before, which had reported a display of war weapons staged on the sea front for munitions workers from all over the country. There were further raids in 1944.

On 1 August 1942, after the worst raid, the *Weston Gazette* headlined its reports and photographs of the local damage with the stirring declaration 'From these ruins a still fairer town shall rise'.

It was some years after the war before the bombsites were redeveloped but post-war Britain saw an infectious optimism for bold redevelopment projects, and a new breed of professional planners who began turning out radical blueprints for our towns and cities. Such a scheme was prepared for Weston in 1947, at the Borough Council's request, by Clough

Williams-Ellis and Lionel Brett. The report was enthusiastic about 'Weston's wonderful assets, some of them unique' but devoted most space to discussing ways of 'consistently and imaginatively exploiting them'.

Very little happened immediately, because of the state of the national economy and difficulties experienced locally in obtaining the necessary war damage compensation.

Lances Corner, opposite the Italian Gardens, saw one of the first projects that revealed the further changes which had come about by this time in building materials and styles. The building line was set back to facilitate road improvements which were anticipated. The Plantation opposite Alexandra Parade was modified to form a giant traffic island, and there were demolitions around Big Lamp corner for redevelopment and road widening. Union Street was widened and rebuilt as a southern extension of High Street. There was considerable opposition to the siting of a new Technical College on the corner of Lower Church Road. The building shocked Westonians by its scale and character. In 1962 the Somerset County Architect said that it would provide 'a really vigorous piece of punctuation in the town scene'.

Perhaps the most controversial redevelopment scheme was the Dolphin Square Shopping Centre between Oxford Street and Carlton Street. There had been some bomb damage but most of this neighbourhood of small streets was still intact. The Council sought to realise here the concept of a conference centre, hotel and covered pool, and commissioned another report, from Chamberlin, Powels and Bon. Investment could not be attracted for the project, however, and the Council switched to a mixture of shops and flats. Existing houses

120 After the first major air raid: clearing up in the Devonshire Road area.

121 Lances' Corner, looking down Waterloo Street across High Street, after the air raid of 1942.

122   The same view from Lances' Corner, looking down Waterloo Street across High Street in 1985.

123   Union Street (now South High Street), looking north, in the 1950s. The scars from wartime bomb damage remained until the 1960s.

124   The Technical College.

125   Houses in Carlton Street, *c*.1960, which were demolished to make way for the Dolphin Square Shopping Centre.

126 & 127   One of the many small streets and courts that adjoined Carlton Street, *c.*1960 and *left*, the Castle Café, a well-known working men's meeting place: a neighbourhood community uprooted for post-war development.

were declared to be sub-standard and clearance orders were obtained; compulsory purchase orders followed, sometimes with minimal compensation. The community was split up and many residents were re-housed on the suburban council estates. They fought a hard and bitter battle, and found a powerful advocate in the Vicar of Emmanuel, the Rev. Ernest Bowes, who said after the fight was lost:

> A decent little residential district has been allowed to become a shambles. Since the blitz I have seen nothing like it ... I hope that the speedy and imaginative development of this area will justify the amount of human suffering to people whose houses have been compulsorily purchased. Otherwise, those responsible will stand morally condemned.

Development projects had been controversial on many occasions in the past, but the enhanced role of the local authority, reflecting post-war notions of planning, seemed to bring the potential for a new bitterness into local disputes.

Before 1939 industry had seemed to be incompatible with tourism, but the wartime policy of dispersing factories to places such as Weston had shown local people that industry could co-exist with resort interests. Local leaders wished to cater for the employment needs of a larger population, and in particular to provide for local school leavers, who found few opportunities in the resort. The wartime factories had adapted to new work. At the Bristol Aircraft factory at Oldmixon a helicopter production line was established in 1956, and in 1961 the site was taken over by Westlands. The Yeovil-based company used the site for the assembly and repair of helicopters and fixed wing aircraft, as well as for the training of pilots for foreign air forces. The company

128   The Westlands Factory in Winterstoke Road.

became the biggest employer at Weston, with 1,500 people at one time working on the 88-acre site. Eventually Westlands bought the Airfield itself, which had continued to operate pleasure flights until 1978. Henly's also had a factory on the site. Both factories, however, were dependent on government contracts, and the town's unemployment problem, while alleviated, remained latent. Westlands ran into a crisis in the mid-1980s. In 1987 the company announced that 800 jobs were to be lost from the 1,200 workforce.

In 1957 Somerset County Council produced a Draft Town Map for Weston. It contained no allocation for industrial development. The Borough Council success-fully sought a change to allow for new initia-tives. Taking advantage of post-war planning legislation, and the lack at that time of restric-tions on local authority spending, the Council obtained loan sanction for developing a new industrial estate at Oldmixon. 130 acres were bought under the Town Development Scheme for an overspill agreement with Birmingham, of which 44 acres were earmarked for industry. Exhibitions were staged in Birmingham in 1959 and 1961. The initiative was a success, and the estate was filled in four years.

In the mid-1960s a second estate of 55 acres was planned, on the other side of Winterstoke Road next to Westlands, but this project became a casualty of the national economic downturn in the late 1960s. C. & J. Clark had opened a shoe factory in Locking Road in 1958, and this was followed by a second at Oldmixon. RAF Locking had become the No.1 Radio School in 1950, and a permanent community sprang up behind the trim hedges along the Locking by-pass, where technicians were trained to work with radio, radar and flight simulators. The Station came to contain the largest complex of training computers in the RAF.

129   The start of helicopter production at Westlands.

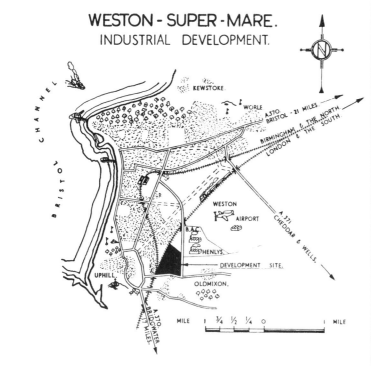

WESTON - SUPER - MARE.
INDUSTRIAL DEVELOPMENT.

KEWSTOKE.
WORLE
A.370. BRISTOL - 21 MILES.
BIRMINGHAM & THE NORTH
LONDON & THE SOUTH
BRISTOL CHANNEL
WESTON
AIRPORT
A.371.
CHEDDAR & WELLS.
B.A.C.
HENLYS.
DEVELOPMENT SITE.
UPHILL.
OLDMIXON.
A.370. TO BRIDGWATER
17 MILES.
MILE ¾ ½ ¼ 0   1 MILE

OFFERS EXCELLENT OPPORTUNITIES FOR THE LOCATION OF
INDUSTRIES IN A MODERN & PROGRESSIVE SEASIDE RESORT.

1.   CONVENIENT ROAD & RAIL ACCESS TO BIRMINGHAM & LONDON.
2.   HOUSES PROVIDED FOR EMPLOYEES WISHING TO MOVE FROM BIRMINGHAM OR OTHER APPROVED
     EXPORTING AREAS.
3.   EXCELLENT LEVEL SITES AVAILABLE WITH ALL SERVICES.
4.   COUNCIL WILL CONSIDER ERECTION OF FACTORY PREMISES TO INDUSTRIALISTS REQUIREMENTS
5.   LOW DENSITY RESIDENTIAL SITES - OWNED BY COUNCIL - AVAILABLE IN A PLEASANT AREA
     FOR EXECUTIVES TO BUILD ON.

130 Advertisement for the Oldmixon Industrial Estate.

131 Houses on the Oldmixon Estate built in conjunction with the new factories.

132 & 133 Clarks Shoe Factory in Locking Road and, *below*, an early view of production, 1958.

Weston had come to terms with a 'mixed economy' of light industry and tourism, and the Council's positive action in the 1960s appeared to be producing an adequate employment base for the local population. No sooner was this goal in sight, however, than it receded again, as new developments unfolded.

The M5 motorway, first proposed in 1961, was constructed between 1968 and 1973, and a new link road from the interchange to the town centre in 1994. In terms of industrial development, however, Weston was not able to realise the potential that the motorway link seemed to promise. There were many other

134   Televisions on sale in a Weston shop, 1957.

towns competing to attract firms that were as well placed by the new system. Hundreds of new jobs were promised by Peter de Savary, who acquired Weston Airfield in 1988, but this scheme for the largest 'brownfield site' at Weston came to nothing and the airfield has been in the hands of official receivers since 1991. Weston never 'took off' as a centre for office development although its population contains thousands of skilled workers who commute to offices in Bristol and elsewhere.

On the other side of the equation, the building of the motorway helped fuel an unprecedented house building boom. Weston had been earmarked by Somerset County Council in the 1960s for major residential growth. The town spread towards the east and the motorway interchange, and the population grew by 20,000 within 15 years. Worle changed from a village, surrounded by deep lanes and ancient farmsteads, to a sprawl of new estates. Many of the new residents were commuters, working in Bristol, Avonmouth or elsewhere. There was much criticism of the planning and layout of the new estates, and of the slow development of neighbourhood amenities. The town increasingly functions as one of Bristol's dormitory suburbs, and the new estates have little organic connection with the old resort.

At the same time the old 'stone town' began to experience difficulties in common with most English resorts. Cheap foreign travel was probably the biggest single factor; more and more people flew to destinations where the sunshine was guaranteed. The resort never acquired the facilities or the hotel accommodation that would have enabled it to cater for major conferences. The polluted state of the Estuary began to attract publicity and criticism. The ending of steamer services at Birnbeck in 1979 removed an attraction which might have increased appeal. The resort became dangerously dependent on a limited section of the tourist market that was shrinking while other sectors dramatically expanded.

135 Trippers arriving at the Locking Road Excursion Platform, 1958.

136 The extension to the Town Hall, 1987.

The last years of the 20th century have seen a growing contrast between new and old Weston. Overall, Weston and the surrounding area is prosperous. There has been significant investment and growth in the retailing and service sectors consistent with rising numbers of commuters and relatively wealthy retired people moving to the town. The Sainsbury store in the District Centre at Worle has been expanded and a large Tesco built in the town centre on the site of the 1860s railway station. Similar 'out-of-town' retail outlets, all with large car parks, have appeared along the motorway link road. In 1992 the Sovereign Centre, fitted between High Street and Victoria Square, opened; initial proposals to attract such a development by offering the Italian Gardens for building (favoured by many politicians and

planners) led to fierce controversy, with the Civic Society raising a petition of more than 8,000 signatures in a fortnight.

Signs of decline in the old resort have grown, however. Annual spending by visitors has continued to fall. It dropped by £21 million in real terms between 1994 and 1998. The last five years of the century saw a drop in staying visitors of 39 per cent. Many former hotels and guest houses, together with other large Victorian private houses, have been converted into hostels, residential homes, drug rehabilitation centres and poor quality bed-sit accommodation. According to the successful bid for government funds made by the Weston Regeneration Partnership in 2000, this has significantly changed the social and economic make-up of the area and led to problems and tensions. The area has the second highest concentration of bed-sits in the UK and 11 per cent of the UK's drug rehabilitation centres. Over 90 per cent of crime in the area is drugs-related. There is a high transient population, and the pupil turnover rate in local schools is up to twice the North Somerset average.

The town centre has experienced 'shrinkage'—a national trend—as smaller businesses have gone under to out-of-town competition and the dominance of a few big national firms; but at Weston the problem has been exacerbated by the decline in tourism. Pedestrianisation of the central High Street came in the 1980s, after much debate, but plans for more far-reaching enhancement and traffic management have remained on paper.

The resort's problems have been only too well illustrated at major seafront sites, which seem to have been left stranded by the ebbing tide of mass tourism. Birnbeck Pier has changed hands three times since 1972 and there have been several redevelopment schemes, all failing to address the significance of a site officially listed as a monument of national importance.

Knightstone Island was put on the market by the local authority in 1986 and leased to Kingfisher (who pulled out in 1991) and to the B.S. Group in 1997. Dr. Fox's Bath House

was restored but the other buildings have so far not attracted investment or imagination.

The Open Air Pool had received a 'makeover' and become the Tropicana in 1983, when the local authority declared that the scheme would soon pay its way. By 2000 it was receiving a subsidy of £250,000 a year. Redevelopment proposals by Mace Estates, including a multiplex cinema and retailing, have not proved popular.

The wider pattern of changes to the old resort's fabric also reveals a loss of direction and identity. The building boom of the early 1970s saw several historic mansions demolished to make way for blocks of flats: the Villa Rosa in the Shrubbery; Glentworth opposite the Marine Lake; Etonhurst in Beach Road; Carlton Mansions, allowed to upstage the *Grand Atlantic Hotel* and a source of widespread dismay. Yet Weston has suffered far less than other major resorts such as Brighton or Torquay in this respect. Far more damage has been done to the resort's character through clumsy alterations and additions to old buildings.

The fight against plans to build 14 storeys on the Etonhurst site was the local conservation movement's first major victory. In 1980 the town's first conservation areas were finally designated and others have followed. There

137 New Hospital at Uphill, 1988.

138   The Civic Society's Heritage Centre in Wadham Street, 1988.

have been notable examples of older buildings being successfully converted to new uses. In 1975 the former Gas Company Offices and Showrooms in Burlington Street became the Museum (the collections had previously been held at the Library), and in 1987 Clara's Cottage was added to show a typical small house as it would have been towards the end of the 19th century.

The Civic Society opened the Weston Heritage Centre in a converted coach house and warehouse in Wadham Street in 1986. From this headquarters the Society has organised several other projects, including the development of the Blakehay Arts Centre in the former Wadham Street Baptist Church and the creation of workshops, a recycling project and a nature reserve in the Town Quarry.

The General Hospital closed in 1986 following completion of a long awaited new hospital at Uphill. In 1991 came plans for demolition and the erection of barrack-like blocks in polychromatic brick, but these were resisted and in 1993 a much acclaimed scheme converting the Boulevard and Alfred Street buildings was completed. Other successful conversions followed at Eastern House in Landemann Circus; at the former British School in Hopkins Street; at the former Royal West of England Hospital (the Sanatorium); and at the former Locking Road Board Schools.

Despite these examples the 'conservation debate' is not yet resolved and local politicians have continued to look to commercial re-development schemes to solve the resort's

139 The Tesco Store in Locking Road, 1988, on the site of Weston's second railway station.

140 Storm damage on the sea front, 1981.

141   The Weston Carnival, 1999. Thousands come to this event every November, the culmination of the Somerset carnival season.

problems. Weston became part of the new District of Woodspring (and County of Avon) in 1974, and the need to centralise staff led to the building of a major extension of the Town Hall, opened in 1980, for which the Albert Memorial Hall behind Emmanuel Church was demolished. In 1996 Avon was abolished and Woodspring became the unitary authority of North Somerset. In 2000 a Weston Town Council was established.

Despite the difficulties there is optimism. North Somerset Council's 'Blue Skies' initiative, which involves wide-ranging consultation on the future of local tourism, has revealed a readiness to look afresh at the role of the resort. Identifying the growth areas in tourism, and playing to its strengths, Weston is setting about charting a new course for the new century—'a seaside destination renowned for its distinctiveness and quality'.

Chapter Nine

Retrospect

A RESORT, LIKE OTHER TOWNS, continues to take advantage of the buildings and amenities won by previous generations, whether or not it is effectively renewing itself. There is thus a factor of 'delayed action' masking the appearance of difficulty, which only the most alert may at first perceive.

In most towns the commercial life in all its aspects is so complex that simple statements about 'rise and fall' are dangerous, but in the case of a resort town like Weston it is possible to describe a clear trajectory of the community's fortunes. The loss of momentum and direction, the disappearance of a clear sense of purpose and identity, which became apparent in the post-war years, probably had their origins in the period between the First and Second World Wars.

Seaside towns can only be fully understood in the context of the wider national story; in themselves they make only partial sense. Resorts are a paradox, whose complete meaning is explained in the history of work although they themselves are dedicated to leisure. The nature of work for most people underwent profound changes in the 19th century, as Britain became the first modern country to exploit new technology and the methods of mass production on a wide scale. The nature of peoples' everyday work influences their whole lives; it determines what they spend most of their time doing, where they live and who they meet; and it determines the character of their leisure. Seaside towns in their developed form were embodiments of Victorian England's leisure options, at first for the upper and managerial classes, later for the mass of ordinary industrial workers. The seaside was the great escape from the factories, mines and offices, of industrial Britain.

The very nature of relief they offered from new forms of work meant that they themselves should contain little industry. The whole point was that they should be different. The conscious decision after the Second World War to attract light industry seems an indication that the pure purpose of the resort was already gone at Weston. Greater mobility and foreign travel, themselves signs that modern work was changing, signalled other leisure options. It is not yet clear whether our resorts have found a role to play in this pattern.

In their heyday, before the First World War, resorts embodied the confidence and optimism of the society they served. In its classic period Weston embodied the fine balance between the natural world and the complex achievements and failures of a technologically advanced society. The pilgrimage to the sea, and the respite from mechanical work, enacted a balance that was crucial in the nation's psyche. Here in physical form was the very meeting place between urban civilisation and the untamed energy of the waves. It was no accident that this became the scene of recreation and refreshment.

At Weston one can still trace, in unusual detail, the outline of the classic watering place.

142   The bandstand in Grove Park.

Seen across the bay from Brean Down the town still looks very much as it did a century ago. The view sums up 'the logic of landscape' as it was interpreted by the mature resort: falling down the hillside and spreading round the shore, the crisp and sharply defined details of a civilised townscape facing out towards the free wild spaces of the Celtic west.

143   Getting a taste of Weston beach.

Select Bibliography

Adamson, S., *Seaside Piers* (1977)

Aston, M., 'Brean Down Fort', Somerset County Council (typescript) (1976)

Aston, M. and Burrow, I. (eds.), *The Archaeology of Somerset* (1982)

Aston, M. and Iles, R., *The Archaeology of Avon* (1987)

Bailey, J., *Weston-super-Mare: The Good Old Days* (1985)

Bailey, J., *Look Back with Laughter* (1986)

Baker, E., *A Chronicle of Leading Events in the History of Weston-super-Mare during the past fifty years* (1887)

Baker, E. (ed.), *John Chilcott's 1822 Guide to Weston-super-Mare* (1901)

Baker, E., *Weston-super-Mare Parish Church 1226 to 1910* (1901)

Baker, E., *Weston-super-Mare: Village Jottings* (1911)

Baker, E., *The History of Weston-super-Mare from 1326* (1912)

Baker, E., *The Village of Weston-super-Mare: Historical Notes* (1928)

Barrett, J., 'A History of Maritime Forts in the Bristol Channel' (typescript in Weston Library, n.d.)

Beisly, P.J., *The Northmarsh of Somerset* (1996)

Billingsley, J., *General View of the Agriculture of the County of Somerset* (1797)

Branigan, K. and Fowler, P.J. (eds.), *Roman West Country* (1976)

Brown, B.J.H., 'Survey of the Leisure Industries of the Bristol Region' (unpublished Ph.D. thesis, University of Bath, 1971)

Buchanan, A. and Cossons, N., *Industrial Archaeology of the Bristol Region* (1969)

Buchanan, B.J., 'The Financing of Parliamentary Waste Land Enclosure: Some Evidence from North Somerset, 1770-1830', *Agricultural History Review 30* (1982)

Burrow, I., 'Brean Down Hillfort, Somerset, 1974', *University of Bristol Spelaeological Society Proceedings 14(2)* (1976)

Coles, J.H. and Orme, B.J., *Prehistory of the Somerset Levels* (1982)

Collinson, J., *The History and Antiquities of the County of Somerset* (1791)

Costen, M., *The Origins of Somerset* (1992)

Coysh, A.W., Mason, E.J. and Waite, V., *The Mendips* (1954)

Davey, N., *A History of Building Materials* (1961)

Day, J., *Bristol Brass: The History of the Industry* (1973)

Dunning, R.W. (ed.), *Christianity in Somerset* (1976)

Dunning, R.W., *A History of Somerset* (1978)

Dymond, C.W., *Worlebury: An Ancient Stronghold in the County of Somerset* (1902)

Evans, J., *Worlebury: The Story of the Iron Age Hill-Fort at Weston-super-Mare* (1980)

Evans, J., 'Mr Pigot's Cottage near the Bristol Channel, Somerset', *Avon Past 3* (1980)

Farr, G., *West Country Passenger Steamers* (1967)

Granville, A.B., *Spas of England and Principal Sea-Bathing Places* (1841)

Gough, J.W., *The Mines of Mendip* (1967)

Hall, W.G. (ed.), *Man and the Mendips* (1971)

Hogg, I.V., *Coast Defences of England and Wales, 1856-1956* (1974)

Hudson, K., *The Fashionable Stone* (1971)

Hutson, A.F., 'The Development of Elementary Education in Weston-super-Mare prior to 1914' (typescript in Weston Library, 1972)

Jackson, W., *Visitors' Handbook to Weston-super-Mare* (1877)

Knight, F.A., *The Sea-Board of Mendip* (1902)

Lambert, D., *Historic Public Parks: Weston-super-Mare* (1998)

Maggs, C., *The Weston, Clevedon and Portishead Railway* (1964)

Maggs, C., *The Weston-super-Mare Tramways* (1974)

Mais, S.P.B., *Walking in Somerset* (1938)

Palmer, W.R., *A Century of Weston-super-Mare History* (1924)

Pawle, G., *The Secret War* (1956)

Pevsner, N., *The Buildings of England: North Somerset and Bristol* (1958)

Pimlott, J.A.R., *The Englishman's Holiday: a Social History* (1947)

Plomer, W. (ed.), *Kilvert's Diary 1870-1879* (1977)

Poole, S., *The Royal Potteries of Weston-super-Mare* (1987)

Rutter, J., *Delineations of the North-Western Division of the County of Somerset* (1829)

Smith, G., *Smuggling in the Bristol Channel 1700-1850* (1989)

Somerset County Council, *The History of Quarrying in Somerset* (1971)

Thomas, D. St J., *A Regional History of the Railways of Great Britain, vol. 1: The West Country* (1967)

Tomalin, D.J., *Woodspring Priory* (1974)

Watts, M., *Somerset Windmills* (1975)

Wickham, A.R., *Churches of Somerset* (1952)

Williams, M., *The Draining of the Somerset Levels* (1970)

Williams-Ellis, C., 'Weston-super-Mare: Post-War Development' (typescript in Weston Library, 1947)

Index